Praise for *Are You Dropping the Baton?*

Dave Harris has produced a timely, highly relevant and challenging resource which integrates theory and practice in a powerful and effective way. There are many critiques of our present system of schooling available but few are based in the deep understanding and practical credibility that Dave Harris brings and the powerful and relevant model that he offers. This is a book that helps extend our understanding of the future direction of education and it is to be warmly welcomed.
John West-Burnham, Visiting Professor of Education Leadership, University of Bristol

Transition is one of the weak points in educational continuity. To anyone considering cross-phase federation as a way of overcoming this problem, this book offers a rationale and plenty of practical ideas to help them on the way. It is rooted firmly in the experience of Dave Harris and his team at Serlby Park.
John Dunford, General Secretary, Association of School and College Leaders

All through schooling is not new. In this authoritative and engaging book Dave Harris makes the case from a historic and international perspective as well as current practice in the UK. What Dave ably manages to do is to present the philosophy of all through schooling then immediately backs that up with a "how to" guide. In one immensely practical book you have all you need to know to be able to work through your own ideas. Then you can use Dave's diagnostics to check out where you are and where you might be headed. Once you have your own plan for the future supported by Dave's ideas and examples and you are just taking a deep breath before the really hard work of implementation, you turn the page and discover a treasure trove of tried and tested activities to get you going. *Are You Dropping The Baton?* is a must have book for schools, federations and Local Authorities even half way thinking of all through schooling.
Deryn Harvey, Director The Innovation Unit

Dave Harris has provided a practical guide for all those wishing to make the journey for our children not only productive with clear outcomes but also inspiring, innovative and enjoyable at whatever age. His bravery and creativity as a leader and educator is matched, nay exceeded, by his own personal example of courage and transformation.
Roy Leighton, Writer, lecturer and adviser/facilitator to organisations and institutions on learning, maturity and creative thinking

The challenges relating to KS3 behaviour and achievement are always high on the list of priorities for school leaders. So often the transition process from primary to secondary school is the key to developing an engaged and happy secondary student. In this book Dave Harris tackles all the issues around transition with an entertaining an informal style that also challenges our thinking. There is a great range of examples and strategies that cover many aspects of school leadership that can help create a school where children really thrive. It includes practical advice about developing an

all through model of education and many case studies of best practice combined with lots of useful resources. A great read that will inspire and enlighten you.
Jackie Beere MBA, OBE, Advanced Skills Teacher, School Improvement Partner, Building Schools for the Future Consultant, Educational Consultant, NLP Master Practitioner, Trainer

Dave Harris, with his usual passionate and forthright style, brings vividly to the attention of the reader issues within our education system which are so familiar they are frequently over-looked. His often humorous approach to these serious issues only helps to illuminate their deep rooted nature and the need for us all to review that which we take for granted with fresh eyes. I sincerely hope that this exciting review of our transition systems will help to ignite a long overdue discussion across the education profession and beyond which will benefit the generations of the future.
Jo Edwards, Headteacher, Moorside Community Primary School

ARE YOU DROPPING THE BATON?

From effective collaboration
to all-through schools –
your guide to improving transition

David Harris
Edited by Ian Gilbert

Crown House Publishing Limited
www.crownhouse.co.uk
www.chpus.com

First published by

Crown House Publishing Ltd
Crown Buildings, Bancyfelin, Carmarthen, Wales, SA33 5ND, UK
www.crownhouse.co.uk

and

Crown House Publishing Company LLC
6 Trowbridge Drive, Suite 5, Bethel, CT 06801, USA
www.chpus.com

© David Harris 2008

Edited by Ian Gilbert

British Library Cataloguing-in-Publication Data
A catalogue entry for this book is available
from the British Library.

ISBN 978-184590081-6

LCCN 2007933488

Printed and bound in the UK by
Athenæum Press, Gateshead, Tyne & Wear

Every effort has been made to trace copyright holders and to obtain their permission
for the use of copyright material. The publisher apologises for any errors or omissions
and would be grateful if notified of any corrections that should be incorporated
in future reprints or editions of this book.

The graphs on page 23 are from The Unfinished Revolution (2001) by John Abbott and Terry Ryan
and have been reproduced with the kind permission of Continuum.

Contents

Foreword by Professor Gervase Phinn

I first met the author of *Are You Dropping the Baton?* when I addressed a large conference of school governors in Milton Keynes and had the daunting task of following his presentation. Here was a speaker of exceptional skill. Dave Harris spoke with passion, a deep and obvious commitment to education, a knowledge and expertise gained from many years in the business, and from establishing and managing a highly successful all-through 3–18 school.

His lecture was far from the dreary wade through depressing overhead transparencies, guidelines and directives that governors frequently have to endure on Saturday morning training sessions. It was energising and uplifting and full of practical advice and good humour. And one should never underestimate the importance of humour. As the great Sir Alec Clegg, the former chief education officer of the West Riding of Yorkshire once remarked, one of the most important characteristics of a good teacher and headteacher is a sense of humour—indeed a sense of fun. It is of inestimable importance, he said, for those who educate the young.

The audience of Milton Keynes governors left that morning in such good humour, wanting to hear much more from this entertaining and motivational speaker, and pressing him for copies of his material. This material, to my delight, has now been developed into an excellent handbook. In this immensely readable and challenging text, Dave Harris offers a range of insights, exciting ideas and practical advice showing how a school might change for the better. He examines with cogency and clarity the problems which have beset education in this country for so many years, the remorseless changes in the school system which have so often depressed and demoralised those in the profession. But he does not dwell on the problems; he moves the reader forward offering clear advice and tried and tested strategies so that those in senior management and governance can effect real change in a school.

So, it gives me great pleasure to recommend *Are You Dropping the Baton?* Everyone involved in the education of the young should have this clear-sighted, persuasive and accessible book to hand.

Professor Gervase Phinn

Foreword by Series Editor, Ian Gilbert

You would think, looking at the make-up of the UK's education system with its patchwork of different schools for different ages, types and classes of learner, of education authorities, inspectors, curricula and examinations, of teachers and teacher training, that it has all arisen out of some well thought-out plan hatched in the minds of great educationalists and dispatched with children's best interests at heart.

You'd think.

When you look, though, at the history of UK education since the Middle Ages[1], what comes through is a hotchpotch of ideas, innovations, reformations and other hopeful or misguided stabs in the dark driven by utilitarian, religious, expedient, prejudiced, occasionally altruistic but often heavily self-serving motives that have led us stumbling towards the current system.

Dividing children—and by logical extension first their classrooms and then their entire schools—by age for the purposes of their instruction is one such avenue down which we have lurched for better or for worse. And, as with all destinations arrived at accidentally, it is always worth standing back and asking the question, do we want to be here at all?

The need to educate children has never been an obvious given. John Amos Comenius, a Czech teacher, scientist and writer who has been dubbed the father of modern education, is quoted as saying:

> Not the children of the rich or of the powerful only, but of all alike, boys and girls, both noble and ignoble, rich and poor, in all cities and towns, villages and hamlets, should be sent to school.[2]

Comenius died in 1670 and, despite the nobility of his claim as we may see perceive it today, the ensuing centuries saw his dream meet with a great many obstructions and objections, notable from the very groups who have ended up in charge of education— the Church and the State.

One such example nearly a century and a half after Comenius is from the Tory MP Davies Giddy who was explaining to the House why he was a tad upset about educational reform:

> Giving education to the labouring classes of the poor ... would teach them to despise their lot in life, instead of making them good servants in agriculture and other laborious employments to which their rank in society has destined them; instead of teaching them the virtue of subordination, it would render them factious and refractory ... it would enable them to read seditious pamphlets, vicious books and publications against Christianity.[3]

---

1 And helping me with my history lesson has been the most informative website put together by retired (and disillusioned) headmaster Derek Gillard: Gillard, D. (2007) Education in England: a brief history www.dg.dial.pipex.com/history/

2 http://en.wikiquote.org/wiki/John_Amos_Comenius

3 Hansard, House of Commons, Vol. 9, 13 July 1807

As society evolved so did the perceived need for the education of young people (although still in no small way driven by the need to have workers with enough literacy and numeracy to be able to operate effectively in the factories and mills without thinking for themselves and messing up the 'industrial method') and, over the last 200 or so years, a great deal of time and effort was put into the publication of various reports about the state of education, the direction it should take and a whole raft of 'big ideas' picked up from one source or another to be tried out, adopted, adapted, distorted or discarded.

One such idea was the development of infant schools, something that came about in effect as a child-minding service that would enable parents to continue working in the cotton mills of New Lanark in Scotland, an idea subsequently transposed lock, stock and teacher to London in 1818. Originally such 'schools' were not so much about formal education and preparation for the next stage of schooling as about teaching children 'whatever might be supposed useful that they could understand, and much attention was devoted to singing, dancing, and playing.' However, the tug of war for children's minds led a Samuel Wilderspin to co-opt such a seemingly wasteful opportunity and introduce more formal instruction to children from the age of two upwards.

That said, the nature of infant education was far more what we would call these days 'child friendly' (or 'trendy, liberal and soft' depending on which paper you read) than that being practised on older children at the time. Here, educational 'pioneers' such as Bell and Lancaster had introduced the 'monitorial method'. This was, in effect, an industrial-age educational process that allowed hundreds of students to be drilled in formal ways using repetitive exercises by a small number of teachers and monitors in a Bible-oriented curriculum based around the three Rs (with a little needlework for the girls and some light gardening for the boys, presumably to relieve the writer's cramp).

The parallel developments in what we know today as secondary education and in infant education left a gap in the last part of our current jigsaw. Primary education was the last piece to fall into place and, here again, we took the magpie approach, seeking out ideas to steal.

1847 saw a book by an Inspector of the Academy of Strasburg translated into English arguing that children should be divided by age for their schooling as a matter of principle: 'Every school, in obedience to this principle, should be divided into two great classes—the one including children from 6 to 9 or 10, the other those from 10 to 14; and it would much subserve many important purposes, if these could be taught in separate rooms.'

Keeping the smaller children away from the older ones was undertaken, primarily at least, so that the youngsters wouldn't disturb their elders. Published in 1871 by the Committee of Council on Education, the *Rules to be observed in planning and fitting up schools* advises that infants need to be taught in a different room 'as the noise and the training of the infants disturb and injuriously affect the discipline and instruction of the older children.'

Another import from north of the border was the thinking of David Stow in the first half of the 19th century who believed that young children learn better as a direct result of interactions with the educated mind of the teacher rather than merely with printed material. Developing a more oral pedagogy entailed smaller classes more finely divided by age and ability and he suggested departmental divisions of children aged 2 or 3 to 6, 6 to 8 or 9 and 9 to 14. These ideas were further developed in 1902 in *Principles of Class Teaching* by a Professor J. J. Findlay where children's development was broken down into stages —infancy (birth to around 4 years of age); early childhood (4 to 6); later childhood (7 to 9); boy or girlhood (10-plus). It was Professor Findlay who pushed forward the idea of the distinct break at age 11 between primary and secondary.

So, after a whistle stop tour of four and a half centuries of education reform and innovation, what did we end up with? A three-part system that provides, at one end, babysitting with musical accompaniment starting from the age of 2 upwards, with formal instruction in the three Rs to provide you with just enough to acquit yourself in your station in life without rocking the boat at the other end, and primary education filling the resulting gap in-between, with children separated by age, by walls and subsequently by location—and a pedagogy being pulled this way and that by the various intransigent advocates of training, child minding, drilling and educating.

Is it any wonder that transition, the process of steering children through the messy battleground of educational maturation, is as Professor Hargreaves of the Specials Schools and Academies Trust calls it, 'The number one challenge currently facing the UK education system.'

And the latest research backs up the fact that we are, in all honesty, still making quite a hash of the whole process:

- 40 per cent of children lose motivation and make no progress during the year after transition.[4]
- Children who were making steady progress in primary school actually go backwards in the first year of secondary school.[5]
- There is a discontinuity between the primary and secondary curriculum, and a lack of information passing between schools relating to pupils' abilities and existing achievements.[6]
- Teachers rarely identified children's individual abilities as making a difference to the transition process, focusing instead on institutional initiatives, an emphasis that carries the risk of creating a degree of helplessness for individual pupils.[7]

However, from the midst of this mess, there is occasionally heard the voice of sanity. A line from the 1931 Hadow Report states: 'A good school is a community of young and old, learning together.'

And if there is one single line to sum up the nature of the book you have in your hands this is it.

What Dave Harris is suggesting is exactly that: in good schools and good schooling there is a genuine necessity to have learners of all ages collaborating in their learning, regardless of what 400 years of often dubious educational innovation may tell you.

---

4   TES, 3 September 1999, research carried out for the NFER (quoted in www.cc4g.net/cms/downloads/File/Public/Transition.pdf)

5   Fouracre, S. (1991) *A case study of the transition from Primary to Secondary School*, Stirling University (quoted in ibid.)

6   Financial Times, 4 July 2002, research carried out by Ofsted (quoted in ibid.)

7   *Negotiating the Transition from Primary to Secondary School*, Zeedyk, S. et al. (2003) Dundee University

What's more, learning science and brain research back this up too. For example, good teachers know that the best way to learn anything is to teach it to someone else. As Virgil said, 'As you teach so you shall learn, as you learn so shall you teach.' Having children of different ages teach each other is of direct pedagogical benefit to all parties. What's more, there is neurological evidence that males who are in contact with young children show reduced levels of testosterone.[8] Spending useful time in the company of young children makes for calmer, less explosive teenagers.

And lumping children together by their dates of birth is too blunt an instrument when it comes to the actual nature of neurological maturation. Piaget's schemata describes transitions in children's cognitive development between the ages of birth to 2, 2 to 7, 7 to 11 and 11 onwards (compare with the stages put forward by Professor Findlay above), yet we also know there can be a two to three year spread in terms of how far an individual's brain has matured compared with classmates of the same age.[9] Furthermore, male and female brains mature at different rates,[10] with girls starting the adolescent stage of maturation earlier than boys on average.

In other words, where is it written that every child is ready to sit that SAT or that exam at exactly the same time on exactly the same day?

Even the idea of the magical age of 16 as the ideal time to examine children and so decide the course and subsequent fate of their entire lives is a practice built on sand not stone. Neuroscience is showing that neurological maturation (and by that we mean the process of 'wiring' up our brains to be at their most efficient; something that starts at the back of our heads as babies with our visual cortex and ends at the front of our heads with the pre-frontal cortex, also known as 'the area of sober second thought') is a process that takes human beings between 20 and 30 years to accomplish. Bear that in mind next time you berate a group of 12 year olds for 'acting childish'.

Doing something because we've always done it that way isn't in itself a justification for dropping it but more often than not in education, the method of 'we've done it that way because we stumbled across it and thought we'd give it a go and now it's stuck' seems to be where so much 'traditional' practice comes from. The demands of the 21st century demand the best possible 21st century education system and it is for educators everywhere to relish the challenge and re-evaluate every aspect of the system that does not add value to educational experience of the child.

With the plethora of options available to every school as detailed by Dave Harris in this book, from affiliations—chewy or otherwise—to full-scale amalgamation, there is no longer an excuse for transition to be hit-and-miss affair it currently is for so many young people.

It's down to you to work out which path you would like to take. And may the 400-year-old spirit of Comenius be with you on your journey …

Ian Gilbert
Suffolk, September 2007

---

8 Meet the Alloparents, Interview with Sarah Blaffer Hardy, *New Scientist*, 8 April 2006
9 *Completing the Puzzle: A Research-based Guide to Implementing the Dramatic New Learning Paradigm* (1996) The Brain Store, CA.
10 *Sex Differences in Brain Maturation during Childhood and Adolescence*, De Bellis, M. et al., (2001) University of Pittsburgh

Acknowledgements

This book is only possible due to some incredible people who have supported me over the years: my wife Esther, whose patience and support has been unfailing; my daughters Bethan and Megan who constantly remind me what it's all about, my parents who always gave me the confidence to believe in myself; Barry, Gary and Steve, who place pupils at the centre of all they do; the staff of Serlby Park for their passion, good will and understanding; Roy Leighton, who helped us realise what was really important; Ian Gilbert and all at Independent Thinking who are on a day-to-day basis challenging the boundaries of education; and Kelvin Peel for his unstinting faith and support.

Thanks also to all those who have so willingly contributed sections to the book: Barry Bainbridge, Hazel Beales, Cindi Chance, Anne Diack, Louise Edwards, Deryn Harvey, Johnny Heather, Chris Hoyles, Susie Kent, Ellen Leese, Joanne McCluskey, Dave McMullan, Linda Orchard, Phil Palmer, Ian Peach, Joy Sweeney, Barry Wyse.

And thanks also to the hundreds of wonderful revolutionaries I have met on the journey.

Vive la revolution!

Introduction

What is this book going to do?

Do not follow where the path may lead.
Go instead where there is no path and leave a trail.

Harold R. McAlindon

From 20 years in secondary education, and more importantly the last four setting up and then running a 3–18 school, I have no doubt that transition is the biggest unsolved issue currently facing education. We are 'dropping the educational baton' for generations of young people.

In this book I will challenge you to consider the extent of the problem we face, to understand how we have arrived at such a situation and give clear practical advice on how you can begin to effect substantial system change.

Along the journey I hope you will have the opportunity to re-think the aims of education and are motivated to develop strategies to improve the relationships between institutions.

Our path is divided into three parts:

Part 1: What is the problem? How did it happen? Why did it happen? Do we really need to change things?

Part 2: How can alternative structures of schooling improve the situation? What are the possible ways of collaborating? Which ways might suit your own situation? Do you really want to change your ways? How can you persuade others that change is needed? How can new ways of leading support change?

Part 3: Examples of transition projects from a variety of schools and situations. How can we start improving relationships? How do we build strong foundations? How do we build new ways of learning? These contain everything from examples which can be delivered in 30 minutes to ones that underpin the work of a whole year.

Please take the whole journey; if the going becomes challenging, stay with it; we are at a point where major change is not only needed, but possible. Collaboration is the key, be it between phases, schools or countries, just give it a go!

Collaborate, collaborate, collaborate!

Part 1

Part 1

What is the problem?

Our 5 year olds enter the education system as a blank canvas and emerge the other end as a confident, well educated young adult—or so the theory goes! Over the past centuries we have allowed ourselves to believe that we have a seamless system which nurtures pupils through this process. We ignore the fact that pupils frequently change school, teacher, environment and methodologies. After all, they are still educated by teachers in classrooms; how much of a problem can that be?

Imagine you are lucky enough to be able to plan and build your own house. You plan the perfect solution to all your needs, a three-storey detached abode of wondrous design. Then you find that the builders in your area have specialised, each company only capable of building one floor. So you engage three companies, one for each floor. Each produces a perfect floor for you.

Sadly, each has produced their own solution to the problems faced. You are left with a building that doesn't work, inefficient plumbing, fittings that don't match, separate heating systems—in fact the house as a whole is a disaster. What kind of crazy world would separate work into such distinct separate units when there was a shared end goal?

Our education system is packed with dedicated professionals shaping the lives of our younger generations, but do they all have the same outcome in mind? This is the key problem in an education system which delivers its information in discrete packages of knowledge. Perhaps the problem is compounded by the fact that we seem unsure as to what our education system is for.

Is it simply an assessment conveyer belt, where progress through the sausage machine is either a 'pass' or 'fail'? It surely must be so much more than this. The picture below should remind us of the issues faced by our system—the development from innocent child is too complex to be left to chance.

Our success will not only be measured in terms of how many GCSEs/A2s our pupil achieves, but on so many other important aspects of their development into adulthood. Eminent people from almost every vocation confidently proclaim that success is so often not a product of examination success, but a direct result of a positive attitude.

If you remain unconvinced try the following activity:

> You have been awarded a six-month all-expenses paid holiday on a tropical island. The only catch is that **you** must choose your replacement—and your pay while you are away and your position on return will depend on the quality of this replacement. You have one week to make the appointment, and only one paragraph to describe the essential qualities for the job. Give it a go, write that paragraph now!

I am confident that almost all of the qualities you describe will be attitudes (hardworking, amusing, loyal, resilient, approachable, etc.) and that you will have made little reference to how many qualifications you require your replacement to have. This confirms the message from business that when appointing, attitude is often far more important than qualifications. It is estimated that 95 per cent of success is due to attitude. Even that icon of intelligence, Albert Einstein, said 'Imagination is more important than knowledge!'

So if our desired output from 11 years of formal education is a complex mix of skills and attitudes, wouldn't it make sense to view these skills and attitudes as a spiralling curriculum rather than as isolated discrete elements taught at separate points of an individual's life?

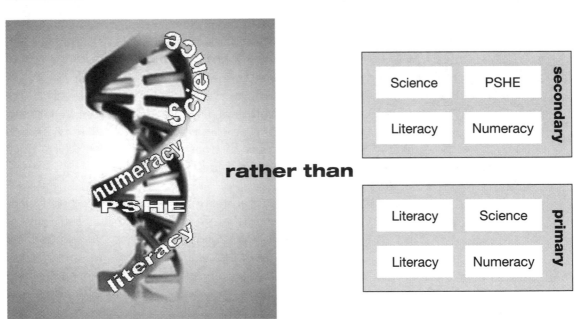

This type of model really emphasises the difficulties faced when separating education into smaller discrete units. Even a lesson on a single objective will cover a variety of strands; multiply that by the thousands of lesson in a year, and the issues of coordinating educational experience become clear.

It may be tempting to conclude that all we need is a national curriculum. Surely if the government sets out everything a child is to learn, it is simply a case of delivering this? If the curriculum was delivered by robots to computers then this kind of logic is fair, but when a diverse range of adults begins delivering in diverse ways to an even more diverse group of children, then logic and cohesion fly out of the window. What has occurred over the years is that primary schools have worked with other primary schools to work out the most appropriate ways to deliver the curriculum; whilst elsewhere secondary colleagues are doing the same. The result is that some very different attitudes have developed between primary and secondary phases, along with an unhealthy mistrust of the work carried out by the other.

As I work with both primary and secondary phases, this has helped me understand the skills of each, and equally to see the differences. Real and meaningful partnership will only occur when there is a much greater understanding between primary and secondary.

Are primary and secondary education really that different? When we first started working on producing an all-age school I thought some things were quite different. I was wrong. Now a few years on I know most things are *fundamentally* different. The rhythms, the language, the approach, in fact the very nature of the phases are as different as any two cousins can be.

The following headings just start to consider the problem.

	Primary	**Secondary**
Parents	At the gate Keen to come into school Prepared to give opinions	Unwilling to become involved Remote from process
Pupils	Involved in day-to-day responsibilities Encouraged to enjoy	Often feel education is done to them Told learning is serious
Class teacher/tutor	A welcoming single point of call, there for instant support and guidance	Often form tutor system involves little more than registering mark
Curriculum	Integrated. Numeracy and literacy often used as tools for delivery. Pupils rarely move	Pupils move around the school to 'experts'. School revolves around the 'god of timetabling'
Differentiation	A key part of almost every lesson. Work is planned at a number of different levels for each topic	Often considered that differentiation is by setting, and a tendency to pitch in the middle
Assessment	On-going formulative assessment, single teacher often able to accurately report to nearest sub-level in a variety of subjects	Assessment often by tests, frequently using a numeric system rather than a criterion-based one. Broad judgments used
Surroundings	Usually vibrant, lively colours with walls containing examples of pupils own 2D and 3D work	Walls often plain (grey or magnolia) with displayed work frequently purchased posters, often unchanged for years

OK, now I can hear the neck hairs starting to bristle on secondary colleagues and blood pressure starting to rise. This may seem a very negative table for secondary, but is it really that unfair? Maybe your school really isn't like this; perhaps you are one of the enlightened few. If you think you are, before you put this book in the 'Books I won't read again' pile, I ask you to give me a chance. Follow one of your Year 7 pupils for a day, then repeat the exercise with a Year 6 in a primary (Appendix A contains a form you may like to use for this activity). Was I that far off the mark? I have spent 20 years in secondary education, and see my own faults all too clearly!

What about a pupil eye's view? The following exerts from Callum's diary are fictitious, but are based on real conversations with pupils either side of the transition barrier.

Callum's Diary

Tuesday 14 March 2006
(Callum is a Year 6 pupil at Little Known Primary)

Dear Diary

It's me again (but I suppose you guessed that). Been another great day at school, being in Year 6 is really the greatest. Miss Smith seems to notice everything we do and even took me to one side to see how Grandad's operation had gone. You know I think she looks more like Hannah Montana off the telly every day.

You know me, Mat, Lucy and Jilly run the healthy eating tuck shop, well today we got our new stock in and we took over £100. Miss Smith was so pleased with what we'd done and didn't even need to check the money, 'cos she accepted we'd got it all right.

In class today it was really good because we finished some work about Africa, after that we had that brilliant man that came in last week. Not only did we get to make those colourful masks we also wrote about it and then Miss Smith got us doing some maths about how much it would cost to make and sell these masks at the Summer Fayre. Tomorrow we've got someone coming from the secondary school, I reckon it's going to be wicked when we go there, it's so big. Anyway I can't keep writing to you all night. Miss Jones gave me some special homework 'cos I need a little bit more work on fractions, must get that done for her, got to keep her happy!

Wednesday 21 March 2007
(Callum is now a Year 7 pupil at Bog Standard Secondary School)

Dear Diary

Tedious or what! Percentages for the gazillionth time in maths today—once we actually got started that is. By the time everybody had got there from PE we were 10 minutes late which of course Miss Sharpe said we had to make up after school, as if it's our fault. We had to count the rubbers in and out and somehow one got missing (I reckon Miss deliberately kept it hidden in the draw of her desk just to make us even later!). Mind you D & T was cool today, we used CAD CAM machinery to make a really good key ring, it was brilliant and looked so good. You know what, Grandad's in hospital again, I wanted to talk to someone, me mates don't understand and I don't know, there's just none of the teachers I really feel I could tell. They're nice enough but who would I tell? Anyway my mates wouldn't think it would be cool to go talking to teachers. Also I really fancy Gina, and I don't want to look like some kind of nerd.

I think I've got some homework tonight which I think is copying out a page from a book (they are really tight at this place—surely it would have been easier just to photocopy it for us!). Anyway I can't find it. Having to lug this bag around to 6 different rooms every day really does me 'ead in. Well diary, I've got to go now, p'raps things will be better tomorrow.

Whilst I quickly admit this is unlikely to rival Adrian Mole, the message is crystal clear—the environment (and the child) can vary greatly either side of transition. The scientific amongst you may be crying out for some greater evidence of the difference. The following questionnaire was sent out to 2,000 pupils across the full range of age groups. A summary of the results are shown by each question. (A copy of the questionnaire can be found in Appendix B should you wish to try this out in your own situation.)

Pupil questionnaire

Year: 1–13 (655 Primary, 782 Secondary)   **Male or Female: F 45% M 55%**

1. How much do you enjoy school?
   (Marks out of 10: 1 = I don't, 10 = brilliant)

   (P) Primary average = 7.8
   (S) Secondary average = 5.3

2. Would any of the teachers at school listen to you if you have a problem?
   (Please tick one box)

❑ Yes	❑ No	❑ Sometimes
P = 59%	P = 0.3%	P = 41%
S = 45%	S = 7%	S = 48%

3. If you have a problem who in school would you go to?

   P = mainly class teacher; S = mix of tutor/friend/specific teacher/head/no one

4. What's the best thing about school?

   Many primary focus on practical lessons, whereas majority of secondary mention a specific subject (Art/PE) or the end of the day/holidays

5. What's the worst thing about school?

   Primary focus on practical issues such as dinner or bullies, while a significant number of secondary mention a specific teacher closely followed by considerable (and probably valid) moans about the toilets

6. Which ways help you most in your learning?

   P = Brain Gym, Thinking Maps, working in twos, teacher telling me!
   S = Practicals, talking, group work, active stuff!

7. How do you think you learn best in school:

	P	S
❑ My teacher telling me	53%	42%
❑ Finding out for myself	41%	34%
❑ Working with a partner	82%	81%
❑ Working with a big group	52%	46%
❑ Working on the computer	74%	70%
❑ Making things	71%	45%
❑ Acting things out	70%	44%
❑ Showing others	42%	22%

   Tick as many as you think are right for you

Please show your no. 1 'best' way with a *

	P	S
❏ My teacher telling me	21%	5%
❏ Finding out for myself	5%	3%
❏ Working with a partner	21%	28%
❏ Working with a big group	6%	9%
❏ Working on the computer	11%	23%
❏ Making things	8%	8%
❏ Acting things out	17%	12%
❏ Showing others	1%	0.5%
❏ No preference	10%	11.5%

8. How often is learning fun? (*Please tick one box*)

❏ Always	❏ Often	❏ Occasionally	❏ Never
P = 34%	P = 40%	P = 23%	P = 3%
S = 6%	S = 27%	S = 64%	S = 3%

9. My teachers try to do the best for me? (*Please tick one box*)

❏ Always	❏ Most of the time	❏ Sometimes	❏ Never
P = 55%	P = 30%	P = 14%	P = 1%
S = 21%	S = 45%	S = 29%	S = 5%

10. How much of a day am I left to work on my own at school? (*Please tick one box*)

❏ Most of the day	❏ ¾ of the day	❏ ½ the day	❏ ¼ day	❏ None of the day
P = 22%	P = 22%	P = 25%	P = 17%	P = 14%
S = 14%	S = 23%	S = 31%	S = 23%	S = 9%

11. If you could improve your lessons in one way, what would it be?

P = more teachers, make it easier, more playtime, bigger play area, better buildings and equipment

S = more fun (by far the greatest number), less writing, longer breaks, less bullying, no uniform, get rid of boring teachers

---

The following to be answered by primary pupils:

If you are a primary pupil, what worries you most about moving to the secondary phase?

Getting bullied, the work, getting lost, stricter teachers, detentions, teachers not believing me, hard work, not being allowed to go to the toilet in lesson time, being picked on, and not making friends, and about 5% declaring no worries at all

What excites you most about moving to secondary phase?

Doing more art, meeting new friends, doing more drama, growing up, more variety of lessons, freedom to walk about between lessons, learning a lot, science labs, harder things to learn and new lessons, with around 8% declaring nothing is exciting them about the move.

The following to be answered by secondary pupils:

What do you enjoy most about the secondary phase?

Being respected by younger pupils, being treated like an adult (mainly post-16 respondents), better school dinners, doing languages, brain testing, better teachers and learning environment, meeting more friends (many answers), pushed more by teachers, and the rather sad response from a year 10: 'You get out of school in Year 11'

What did you prefer about the primary phase?

Break times, easier work, less pressure, got on better with the teachers, smaller and more intimate, less homework, less strict, more fun, teachers knew who you were, toilets were always open, and the very practical: 'Not having to carry your bag around'

The results will shock few who have spent any serious amount of time in both primary and secondary education, but the pupil voice helps clarify the issues. It is obvious that much of the 'drift' in attitude will be a result of raging hormones and the change to adolescence, but a series of issues spring form the results:

- A need to improve pupils' enjoyment of secondary education
- A need to increase secondary pupils' level of trust in their teachers
- Pupils' perception of their own learning strengths may not match those of their school
- Practical issues in the new school are the major cause for concern for primary pupils
- Increased freedom and the desire to 'fly the nest' dominate primary positive attitudes about transition
- Worries about bullying are great for primary pupils, but are rarely mentioned as an issue by secondary ones. Secondary pupils view their primary time in a nostalgic way remembering the relationships and break times

Before trying to read too much into the pupil perceptions, it is important to consider other points of view. The problem is, I was trained for secondary. I worked for 20 years in secondary, and sadly must have developed a warped viewpoint in this time. Convinced as I am of the need for change, I must ensure that I see the educational world as clearly from the primary viewpoint. Therefore one step was to undergo a series of interviews with primary headteachers, the results of which, shown below, stiffened my resolve to lead a transition revolution.

Thank you to the following for giving of their valuable time (which reminds me, can anyone tell me why primary heads have less support than secondary ones and therefore work harder, but get far smaller wages?): Steve Dent (St Patricks); Geoff Ingman (Misson), Steve Cattle (Newbald Primary); Liz Piddington (Blyth), Kerrie Clowes (Harworth Church of England), Jo Edwards (Moorside Primary, Halifax).

1. What are the strengths of primary education?
- Knowing every child and parent
- Staff together in single staff room
- Fun and excitement (even with the literacy and numeracy strategy)
- More good teaching than ever before
- Excellence and enjoyment. Family environment. Children arrive at 3 into a parenting environment. Foundation of skills for life.
- Exciting, flexible enjoyable lessons not so dominated by syllabus, until Year 6 where the lessons become prescriptive
- Subject knowledge—National Curriculum work has taken specific knowledge to a younger age
- Increased technical vocabulary
- Primary age a magical age where children are still ready to learn
- As a smaller organisation quicker to instigate change

2. What are the weaknesses of primary education?
- Teaching to the tests—too exam focused
- Starting tests too early
- Government focus on assessment and league tables. Initially these helped standards—now gone too far. Too much literacy and numeracy at the cost of everything else—a straight jacket
- Very lonely as a head
- Writing doesn't have enough time
- Dynamics of having fewer staff
- The central nature of the head
- A weak teacher in primary affects the same child all day every day
- The inevitable pressure created by LEA/DFES (league tables) which we seem unable to shake off
- Inadequate science/technological equipment
- Everything is focused on the primary headteacher
- Some teachers and schools become too set in their ways

3. What are strengths of secondary education?
- Structure—most 11 year olds look forward to coming and having new subjects
- Specialist subject knowledge of teachers is greater
- Makes the children into young adults. Picking up gaps in expertise

- Weak teachers are not so damaging to an individual pupil
- Ability to offer specialist teaching and equipment
- Flexibility and bigger budget
- Focused work covering pre planned syllabi
- Expert subject teachers rather than 'Jack of all trades'
- Specialist room facilities and resources
- Great range of knowledge and expertise and experiences within premises
- High turnover of staff

4. What are the weaknesses of secondary education?

- Don't know the children as well. Parents say, 'I saw six teachers last night, I don't think any of them knew who my child was'
- Kids say, 'We are doing what we did last year!'
- Secondary staff not aware of how intensive Year 6 is—compared with a relaxed Year 7
- Very exam (academic) focused—need more relevance to all studies
- Not accepting the levels children reach in primary schools. Occasionally with good reason, but not always so!
- Being inflexible with progress of work, often not knowing what primaries do. It is more impor tant that secondaries know what we do than vice versa! (However, good primary teachers are eager to know what their pupils will be doing next!)
- Pastoral care? Parents feel they do not have a proper route into school
- Too much repetition of Year 6 work

5. What does good transition look like?

- Excited and enthusiastic children looking forward to going to a safe place they already know and have happy experiences of
- Not scared—familiar, know staff and other pupils
- Interplay between both schools. Visits of staff and pupils between both schools
- Year 6s fully aware of what awaits them. No hidden surprises. Informative meetings and literature
- Primary takes the best practice from secondary and vice versa
- Teachers from secondary spend time with primary pupils and staff and listen to the profes sional views of primary colleagues
- More pupil visits to secondary school site—with and without parents
- Bridge building days
- Starts in September prior to the move—all dates for the year in a nice booklet—well pre sented. Communication must be good
- Secondary staff should come and observe primary teaching
- Secondary should deliver lessons in primary and then pupils also go to secondary
- Visit to talk about all children, not just SEN
- Even if primary school only sends one child secondary must visit and get involved

6. When transition goes badly what are the characteristics?

- Transition/bridging activities are planned—carried out by primary then sit on secondary shelf (most had examples of this!)
- Primaries often feel information and knowledge is not used
- Lack of understanding between phases
- People not going to their catchment area schools
- Parents not knowing what to expect. A lack of correspondence, communication, etc. Frightened children not knowing what to expect. Fearful parents being daunted

- Subject expertise is ignored. Testing is ignored
- Avoid last minute work. Just because July suits secondary doesn't mean it's the best time!
- Use information (pastoral and academic) from primary
- Use primary information to help groupings and avoid exclusions

7. How do you think transition could be improved?

- More onus on parents to push themselves forward at primary and better communication with them
- By consulting all parents with 'openness' and 'frank' discussions
- Questionnaires, DVDs of school day, activities, teachers introducing themselves
- Tours of school frequently, not just prior arranged. Lots of parents seeing the school at work
- More visits/activities like the School Sports Co ordinator
- More integration—more staff visits, more pupil visits
- Don't take CAT testing (or any other external test, NFER, etc.) as gospel
- After SATs primary pupils should spend much more time in the secondary site (one/two days)
- Transition projects are often half hearted—need following through

What struck me was the passion and understanding shown by primary colleagues. Most understood why transition often fails; but they were not looking to blame, just to find solutions.

One man who has experienced transition from a perspective few other teachers have is Barry Shackley. Barry was Head of North Border Junior School in Bircotes, North Nottinghamshire for 20 years before playing a key part in the amalgamation to form our all-through learning community, Serlby Park. For the past 12 months he has been situated on the secondary site as Vice Principal of Innovation. Barry has had to make the same transition as that made by thousands of Year 6s. The experience of fitting into a different way of doing things has shocked the usually self-confident Shackley.

'A change is as good as a rest'—don't you believe it. Change is anything but! How about change as unnerving, frustrating, intimidating, rejuvenating and always challenging. Having been the headteacher of a successful junior school for 20 years, in September 2006 I left my 'comfort zone' behind and relocated to 'the comp', as locals call it, but which is in reality the second ary phase of our new 3–18 school. A change of title to Vice Principal (Innovations) left everyone bemused and probably amused as the dinosaur from down the road moved in. But what was I moving into? I felt much as a Year 7 pupil must feel as they cross the threshold to secondary education; overawed and bewildered by the magnitude of my ignorance of this new environment. The analogy has proven to be quite profound and I have gained great insight into the challenges faced by young people as they move into secondary education.

It was an inauspicious start, with no office for over half a term, having been used to my own for 20 years, where everyone knew where I could be found or at least leave a message knowing I was bound to touch base at some point. I was used to having everything I needed to hand to function effectively and now I was living out of a briefcase, boxes and bags that I was transport ing from the boot of my car daily to work in any corner that I could find. This was frustrating and difficult to establish a routine, and this is a feeling experienced by all primary pupils on transition. They too are used to touching base and having all their resources around them and now they have to plan whole days at a time and carry everything with them to the four points of the com pass ... and where is room D12 anyway?

Routines, procedures and protocols have taken some grasping and I have been suitably chas
tised for not keeping the appropriate people informed of my actions. In fact, letting staff know
in secondary school is such a big task and you're never sure that you've reached everyone you
should—somewhat different to 'popping around classrooms' in the juniors and sticking your
head in the door to pass on a message in the full knowledge that everyone has received it within
10 minutes. How long does it take young people to come to terms with the new rules and regula
tions pertaining to secondary school life and who do they go to if they need clarification, when
they no longer have access to a class teacher all day? How frustrating and disappointing is it
also if the member of staff they ask does not have the answer because it is not within their area
of responsibility?

Expectations take some living up to. As a junior school head, I had clear expectations of staff
and they of me, but what of secondary staff expectations? What are they? Are they appropriate?
Can I deliver? I'm still working on this and forever will be, but it can be disconcerting. It affects
self esteem if you think you might not be doing what others expect of you, and with so many
more staff in multifarious and often very focused roles rather than the generic roles in primary, it
is a big challenge!

Our youngest pupils have also to come to terms with this as they move from teacher to teacher,
across a full range of subjects, each with their own set of rules and expectations. How flexible
and resilient do they have to become in order to cope with the differing demands? I'm certainly
getting an idea of the kind of preparation young people need in order to help them in this key area
of secondary school life.

And what of the heartbeat of the school community—the pupils themselves? How worrying is
it for the youngest pupils in secondary school when they meet with older students at break and
lunchtime? How will they be treated by them? Have they anything to fear? Will they be subject
to physical or verbal abuse? I am sure for many it can be an uncomfortable part of the school
day especially in the early weeks of the new school year. My own experience mirrors in part that
of Year 7. Fortunately the vast majority of the older students are known to me from their junior
school days but I would be lying if I didn't admit that a crowd of Year 10 or 11 students can
appear quite intimidating, especially when engaging in horseplay or lively banter. When talking
to adolescents one has to be careful of tone and manner, otherwise their response can be surly
or even provocative. They can be more argumentative and defiant and have a stronger sense of
justice and fairness than younger pupils, which can be intimidating to staff. I am comfortable with
older students but I can fully appreciate anxieties that younger pupils may have in their relation
ships with them in the early days.

So what contributions have I been able to make within the secondary phase as Vice Principal
(Innovations) given my primary background and experience of 20 years leadership? Firstly I have
supported the implementation of a cross curricular approach to learning during the first two peri
ods of each day with form teachers. This has not only enabled us to build a primary approach
to teaching and learning but also provide social and emotional support for pupils through a key
teacher every day, not unlike their previous class teachers. Pupil rewards for work, effort and
behaviour have been transferred from the primary phase and a weekly year assembly led by me
have helped foster a 'Year 7 identity'.

In teaching Year 9 set 4 for mathematics I have been able to use a primary approach akin to
the numeracy strategy at KS2, which is proving successful, and so I am looking to support

secondary colleagues with their practice with lower attainers, especially in those subjects which set pupils according to ability.

Because of my unique experience of having been headteacher to 70 per cent of the pupils in the secondary phase, and therefore enjoying positive relationships with them, I manage the school's mentoring system for Year 11 students. I mentor five students myself and support colleagues in mentoring other challenging students. This year we are developing a more integrated mentoring system based upon monthly mentor meetings supported by performance data in order to focus on raising standards alongside personal development and individualised learning.

What have I learned by transferring to our secondary phase? Well I have learned that working with adolescents can be very challenging and my respect for secondary colleagues has grown. I have reinforced my belief that there is a need for a continuum of learning from primary to second ary and that younger pupils benefit from a modified curriculum to support this. Colleagues in all phases have so much to learn from each other and it is vital that an environment is created to facilitate this process to develop their pedagogy.

Finally, in order to fulfil my role as Vice Principal (Innovations), according to the Oxford English Dictionary, I need to bring in new ideas and methods. So what better starting point could there be than to move the dinosaur out of his comfort zone and see what change can do for him and the school.

No matter which of the sources is taken, the message seems the same: some major smoothing work needs to be done at the intersection between the primary and secondary phases if we are not to continue losing valuable chunks of education time in the process.

How did it happen?

Surely there must be some good reasons why we separate into primary and secondary schooling?

Interestingly it seems that there are no compelling educational reasons for separation, but many practical reasons that have shaped the current system that we accept as normal. One hundred years ago, it was common to educate pupils from 5 to 15 in the same school, often the same room. This model flourished not just in Britain, but in many parts of the world. While presenting at an iNet conference in Georgia I had the privilege to spend time with the Dean of Education at Southern Georgia University, Cindi Chance. Cindi is one of those enthusiastic people who positively influence thousands of teachers each year. She became even more animated when I discussed the issue of transition. She told me of the current resurrection of interest in the 'one-room classroom'. Her eyes glazed.

"The mention of the one-room school likely conjures up memories of Laura Ingalls Wilder and the Little House on the Prairie television series. Today's educators and youth would express concern for those who attended, when in fact many students who attended one-room schools are now leaders of countries, company executives, successful professionals, inventors, leaders of school reform in the twenty-first century, and other major contributors to life as we know it today. I am sure there are lessons to be learned from the one-room school model!"

With little persuasion, Cindi agreed to research the issue further and write a piece for this book. She agreed to elaborate on the one-room model of schooling to try to help us understand how it came about and why it went away. She wrote this article along with Dr Brent Thorp, Dr Fayth Parks and Dr Meng Deng.

The One Room School

Though thoughts of one room schools are often associated with fascinating stories in literature by such writers as Walt Whitman, W. E. B. Dubois, Washington Irving and Stephen Crane, and are associated with well known tales such as the Legend of Sleepy Hollow, The Adventures of Tom Sawyer, The Hoosier Schoolmaster and the Goosepond School, these schools were real. They existed throughout history internationally and many schools remain scattered throughout the world today. The impact of the one room schools on our country is recognized by the US government. In April 2002, the US Secretary of Education, Rod Paige unveiled the new look of the US Department of Education in Washington DC. Both entrances to the building host a façade of a one room school. Dr Paige (CSAA, 2006)[1] explained that the entrances '... are a reminder that we do not serve a faceless bureaucracy or an unchangeable system. We serve an ideal. We serve the ideal of the little red schoolhouse. It [one room school] is one of the greatest symbols of America—a symbol that every child must be taught and every child must learn, that every community was involved and every parent's input valued. Those little schools were built to serve a need: to equip children for the future as citizens and workers.'

---

1 County School Association of America (CSSA) (2006), http://csaa.typepad.com/country_school_associatio/2006/09/index.html

Though the schools have diminished in number their impact remains. Such schools still operate in the United States, Australia, China and many other countries, primarily in isolated rural or moun tainous areas, the outback, and on the open plains areas. Worldwide one room schools share some common characteristics—poorly funded, limited teaching resources, and one teacher who serves as the principal, teacher, janitor and community liaison (Cordier, 1998).[2] Examples of this sameness could be included from many countries, however, we chose to provide examples from two very different countries—the United States and China.

In the rural areas of China, there are three types of elementary schools: centre school, village school, and 'teaching point' school (Li, 2005).[3] A centre school is often located in the township that consists of 10–15 villages. Centre schools are generally not one room schools. They include all elementary grades—1 to 6. They also have access to additional resources so that vil lage schools and teaching points (in its catchment area) can be supported. For some small villages and especially those in mountainous, remote or extremely poor areas, one alternative for education is the teaching point catering to the younger chil dren and providing for the lower grades—generally Grades 1 to 3. For Grade 4 onwards children will travel further to a larger village with a village school that offers all primary grades. Below are pictures of some of the one room schools in operation today. As with the one room schools in the US and other parts of the world, the teacher is responsible for all the roles necessary to operate a school—the principal, teacher, leader of the social and cultural experiences for the area, and often the janitorial and maintenance staff (Lin, 2003).[4]

The school below in Guizhou province might make students and educators of today wonder about the community's commitment to education. However, its existence reflects the same advocacy for education exhibited by poor families in the rural south after the Civil War. The Chinese characters on the building say: 'Basic education is the foundation for the realization of the goal of developing a nation by science and education' (Deng, 2003).[5]

[This makes an interesting alternative to the UK's 'Success for all!']

Though one room schools are still scattered nationally and internationally, in order to re live the life span of the one room school model it is necessary to focus the discussion on one very limited area—one room schools in the state of Georgia, USA. The one room schoolhouse was a ubiquitous feature of the rural Georgia countryside from the late nineteenth century to the mid twentieth century. It was the mainstay of the state's

2 Cordier, M. (1998) *Schoolwomen of the prairies and plains.* Milwaukee, WI: Rethinking Schools Ltd.

3 Li, L. & Xu, T. (2005) Yi ren cheng qi yige xuexiao [One man and one school]. Available online at: www.southcn.com/news/community/shzt/teacher/work/200511030360.htm (accessed on 18 February 2007).

4 Lin, R.Z. (2003) Minban jiao shi [People-run teachers]. Available online at: www.edu.cn/20010830/210094. shtml (accessed on 18 February 2007).

5 Deng, H. (2003) Implementation of Policy on Inclusive Education in Rural and Urban China (Hong Kong PhD thesis preserved in the University of Hong Kong.

public education system. They stood at crossroads and in groves dotted across the counties. At their peak there were more than 7,000 one room schools in the state of Georgia. As consolida tion and funding grew dramatically after 1950, the buildings quickly began to disappear. Most were allowed to simply collapse from neglect and disuse. Others were converted and expanded to other uses including homes, churches or most often storage buildings for farms, since most were very rudimentary buildings in the first place. Today, only a handful of one room schools are preserved across the state.

It is important for us to recognize that this model of education came about through lack of money, but not to assume that the outcomes were poorer for this. Historical, cultural and eco nomic circumstances created distinct settings for rural education. In addition to learning centres, many one room schools were social gathering places, such as a public meeting space, that strengthened cultural, political and social identities. Communities were tied together via local histories and collective values. Though excited about the 'new brick school era' that emerged with the funding of school transportation and new consolidated schools, many black families and poor white families experienced a social and cultural loss as one room schools disappeared. No longer did each community have its own 'gathering place', its social, political, and cultural cen tre. This, many believe, was the beginning of efforts to involve parents in the schooling of their children. The effort to involve the entire community in the commitment once associated with the one room school—that education is the responsibility of the entire community, not just the par ents—is an ever increasing challenge to education and educators.

This background has a resonance with the development of single-room schooling in the UK. Both my own mother and grandmother spent time in a one-room school. My grand-mother knew nothing else, often talking with happiness of her years huddled around the single stove in the centre of the room of the tiny school of Neen Sollars. The model was a result of necessity, as was the requirement of older children to deliver the work to the younger ones. So I asked Cindi if there was anything we can learn from the one-room school.

Fundamental characteristics of one room schools such as aspects of teaching, multi age class rooms, peer support and interdisciplinary projects are identified as educational approaches being copied in large systems across the country. General curriculum studies and character education are noted as important features of rural schools missing from today's education.

As we look at the one room school, there is no intent to imply its effectiveness for today's world. However, there are recurring themes and models that parallel many current research based recommendations to address challenges linked to present day needs for increased student achievement. These themes include multi age grouping, peer support and interdisciplinary projects—but also school improvement initiatives such as non graded schools, project based instruction, character education and inclusion of all learners into regular classrooms.

Educators are beginning to question scripted curricula and mandated teaching strategies and models. Most educational reformers are challenging these 'one size fits all' programmes imposed on schools. The call for returning to programme models that meet the needs of individual stu dents, schools and communities seems to be a call to revisit some of the teaching strategies used in the one room schools.

Out of necessity, not research based or mandated, teachers in the one room schools used multi age groupings, peer tutoring, inclusions of children with special needs and non graded models.

Present research and common sense informs us that the best and deepest learning comes from application of learning to real life situations. The teacher in the one room schools, by necessity, used peer tutoring and multi age grouping in order to cover the content and skills needed for all ages assigned to the school. These sometimes included as many as eight to ten grade levels with ages from 4 to 16. Teaching the content to lesser skilled peers or younger students served as a real life application of the learning and therefore strengthened learning. The lesser skills readers were 'included' in the daily lessons by single or group recitations, choral reading and by assigning duties to teach the students to be a productive member of the group (bringing in water, maintaining the fire, recess duty, watching younger children).

I attended a small rural school and remember vividly a student with special needs who was assigned such duties. He was likely 15 or 16 years old and still attending the elementary school. He was assigned 'listening to the little ones read' duty, water and [outside] toilet supervision duty, as well as supervision of the little children in the playground. I don't think any of us really realized his limitations. To us he was a productive and valued member of the school family (who just happened to be younger than the teacher but old enough to experiment with chewing tobacco when the teacher wasn't looking). After the 'red brick new school era' arrived, he was no longer allowed to be a part of the school family. He became lost in a community that no longer needed him.

Project based instruction, hands on/discovery learning and interdisciplinary project models are being reintroduced as a school improvement strategy. In the one room school, these models resulted not from a research base that supported their use, but from the lack of purchased materials available to the teacher, and a very limited time to teach multiple subjects to multiple age groups.

Another factor that supported this interdisciplinary projects model was the community expectation that the school would prepare young people for life skills and work. The hands on interdisciplinary projects often focused on applying rote learning of literature, mathematics, etc. to real life problems— understanding of farm plants and animals, financial examples such as predicting yield of farm crops, ability to determine 'board feet' from standing trees, distance and travel time between locations needed for materials and supplies, marketing locally produced products, Bible study related to maintaining social norms and mores, etc. The community expectations for the school focused on producing educated leaders to ensure personal and community growth and prosperity.

Many state and national mandates tout content mastery followed by standardized testing as critical to school renewal/improvement. One room schools modelled content mastery as its goal, however, in most cases followed by authentic assessment methods and re teaching, peer tutor ing, etc. when needed. These resulted in the one room school because of the schools' connec tions between assessment and community involvement and expectations. Parents who made the sacrifice to keep children in school expected them to learn, that the learning be witnessed by the community, and that the learning would benefit the larger community. Examples included spelling bees, maths bees, projects, performances for families, Bible study for the ministry, train ing of new teachers for growing communities, local political leaders and advisors, etc.

The message seems clear: whilst a return to everyone being educated in the same room is impractical, the benefits of this system should not be lost on us. Perhaps with today's high-speed broadband accessing personalised learning platforms, the one-room idea can be approached from a global perspective—not confined by bricks and mortar, but only by imagination.

Imagination? Now there is something too frequently missing from the organisers of cur rent education!

Why did it happen?

Now that is a good question, and like most good questions there is no one simple answer. Why have we developed into specialised educational 'experts', seemingly unable to share our knowledge effectively? I believe a number of factors must be at the heart of it: standards, curriculum change, efficiency, improved funding, globalisation, communication and increased mobility, to name but a few. Let's take a few moments to explore each in turn, and how they may affect our diary boy Callum.

Standards

Central government want to know how well Callum is doing at school and, perhaps more importantly, how well his school is doing. The concept of national guidance rears its head. The locally based one-room school is required to compete on the standards agenda with larger town based schools. Softer skills are given a lower status, with the recall of specific packets of knowledge placed as the key measure of success. Accountability becomes the new word; schools are encouraged to improve their own standards by whatever method they can. Communication between schools becomes a distant memory, 'Why should I worry about how Callum does in his next school? I only get judged on his success now!'

Curriculum

Callum wants to learn all the latest subjects. The curriculum has become even more intricate; new levels of expertise are required in a larger variety of subjects; the army of generalists are replaced by specialists. Specialists feel 'wasted' delivering more general subjects so offer their specialism to a wider range of pupils and schools. The knowledge is packaged in age-related chunks, with 'the basics' allocated to the younger years, ideal for delivery by the generalist.

Efficiency

Public services become more accountable, tax becomes the issue on which elections are won and lost. Education becomes a political football. Why have many small schools, when fewer big ones will be cheaper? 'Specialism = efficiency' comes the call.

Improved funding

With the increased focus on education, more funding does come available. A focus is made on the quality of the buildings required to deliver a modern education. The concept that top quality education requires top quality buildings is often warped into the incorrect 'top quality buildings produce top quality education'. Somehow the focus on providing wonderful science laboratories did not produce equivalent jumps in the standard of the education occurring in them. For a while, education lost its understanding that the key ingredient of education is learning rather than schools. Then when schools *are* allowed to develop innovative learning centres, they are usually local responses, and two neighbouring schools can look and feel very different. Callum may spend his primary years in a bright, colourful, modern primary, only to transfer to a 20-year-old secondary school, completely alien to the learning techniques adopted in the primary.

Globalisation

The ability to communicate around the globe, with the increased knowledge that results, is a wonderful thing. However it brings with it pressures. Suddenly we are all competing in a global marketplace. Suddenly the outcome of every 7 year old is under scrutiny. 'Are we falling behind?' comes the cry. The pressure builds—the very thing that could offer salvation and innovation becomes less likely. 'Callum is competing against young children from all over the world—he must learn more'; but Callum must *want* to learn more, and there is the heart of the problem.

Communication

The variety of ways to communicate has improved beyond imagination over the past 100 years, but has this been matched by a similar improvement in our communication? I fear not! Receiving 50 e-mails a day may have increased the number of communications, but it has not improved the quality. For effective communication, time and attitude are essential—both of which are sadly missing from relationships between schools. When Callum is represented to his new secondary school as a series of letters and numbers, can we be surprised that he feels less than positive about his new environment? Electronic communication too frequently focuses on levels and facts and, important though they are, they should support the development of a relationship, not be the basis for it.

Increased mobility

This is another case where a 'good thing' can have a restricting effect on the education system. The danger can be that increased mobility is used as a reason for developing an age-guided solution to education. 'It's spring, Callum is 11, he must be learning about elements.' The temptation is to assume that the stress of starting a new school is removed by a common organisation, when actually a common approach to emotional intelligence may offer more support for the individual.

Thinking back to the lessons we can learn from our example of the one-room school: this was in a time when schools were a local resource and served discreet communities. As greater numbers of students required educating to higher levels in different subjects, the desire for specialist teachers arose, from which grew the larger secondary school. This split was to develop into a yawning cavern as the secondary school was encouraged to believe that secondary specialism meant an excellence in education, and the primary 'holistic' approach was somehow less essential. Primary education became undervalued compared to secondary, and despite many public celebrations of its successes, it still remains very much the poor relation with regard to funding. Take the following examples for two similar sized schools:

Big Primary (600 pupils aged 4–11)
Small Secondary (600 pupils aged 11–16)

School budgets are calculated from a variety of single grants (always greater for secondaries than primaries) plus an amount for each pupil (AWPU = age weighted pupil unit). AWPUs change between local authorities, but as can be seen in the fictional example below from www.teachernet.gov.uk, secondary aged pupils obtain greater funding than primary.

Reception	2,199
1	2,199
2	2,199
3	2,241
4	2,241
5	2,241
6	2,241
7	3,100
8	3,100
9	3,100
10	3,100
11	3,128

So Big Primary would receive about £1.3 million from the AWPU plus other grants (e.g. personalisation, standards fund, devolved capital), whilst Small Secondary would receive £1.8 million plus similar grants to the primary—but each being higher.

This poses an interesting question: both schools educate the same number of pupils, both will employ a similar number of teachers, both require specialist resources, so why the great difference in funding? This is particularly interesting when it is remembered that older pupils are supposed to develop greater independence! With this difference in mind, the varying approaches to leadership between the phases can be understood. The less power devolved away by the head and the smaller leadership teams of the primary are not a product of a difference in philosophy, but a result of a shortage of funds.

John Abbott, in his excellent book, *The Unfinished Revolution*, demonstrates a similar point using the graphs reproduced on the opposite page.

If funding is not based on physical/educational need, then how can we be surprised when schools simply reflect this mismatch in funding?

So it should not surprise any of us that individuals in both primary and secondary schools view each other with suspicion. The idea of a common team united in the development of individuals has become a fantasy. The difference in self-perception within primary and secondary schools can probably best be shown by asking a teacher to answer the following question, 'What do you teach?' The secondary answer will be Maths, English or similar, whereas the primary response will be 'children'. This simple demonstration summarises the problem we currently face.

Intellectual weaning based on normal human development

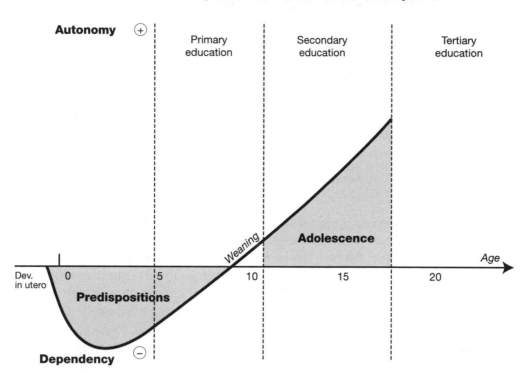

Current relationship of expenditure to class size

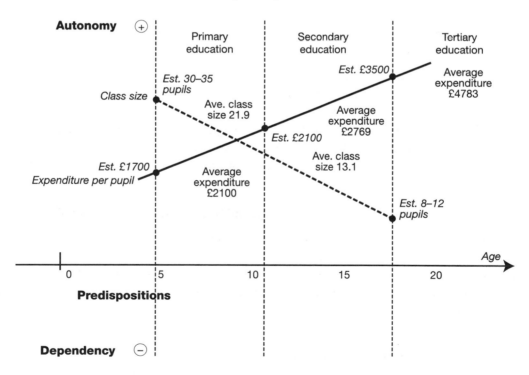

Figures are for England and Wales and come from *Education at a Glance: OECD Indicators 1997*

By kind permission of Continuum

Do we really need to change things?

A thought popped into my frequently empty mind: what does the brain tell us about transition? Maybe the separating of education into fragments is to help us learn. Perhaps the neurons fire more efficiently when stimulated in these different ways. I decided to ask a friend of mine, Dr Andrew Curran, a consultant paediatric neurologist at Alder Hay Children's Hospital in Liverpool, and a man who has forgotten more about the brain than I will ever know.

Are there neurological reasons for the different approach between primary and secondary?

Brain development is essentially a continuum from conception to death, with the main develop ment in most people being mostly completed by the age of 25. There are, however, big changes around the age of 10 when the child moves to Piaget stage 3. This reflects the significant neu rochemical changes occurring in the brain around this time relating to the relative activity of dopamine—its relative activity increases. This is to optimise learning in the frontal brain—and this is presumably to meet the needs for social learning that teenagers are driven by. It increases risk taking activities and predisposes them to dysinhibition. In my opinion, therefore, teaching should progressively change as the child moves from early teenage to early adult, but this is more to do with giving the growing and maturing brain the room to develop in a safe environment —one which encourages experimentation. The change in teaching style should therefore be a gradual continuum to reflect the increasing maturity of the individual. Obviously, central to this should be a strong core focus on emotional learning and literacy. As you know, I believe that this should be central to all school learning.

To what extent is the brain flexible enough to cope with the changes between primary and secondary?

This will very much depend on the individual—the more 'social communication disorder' they have (and one world expert puts the rate of social communication disorder as high as 35 per cent of all children), then the more emotionally immature they will be and the less able to deal with change effectively. I am a strong supporter of keeping children in their present year for an extra year to allow emotional growth to proceed in an environment where they can succeed emotion ally. This is particularly important in 8 to 11 year olds. The step from Piaget stage 2 to 3 is large.

How does the brain protect itself from huge differences in teaching styles?

The answer to this is simple—disengagement and behavioural problems. An inability to cope with change is probably around the answer to the previous question, i.e. their brain is just not old enough to achieve the extra sophistication required to make the step. Hence, the answer to your first question—it should be a continuum based around encouraging healthy emotional growth, not an abrupt change.

Does self-belief help the brain work better?

I believe so, provided it is based on reality and is not delusional! At the end of talks on the neu robiology of learning I always try to remind people: If a child is in an environment where they feel understood as a person, then their self esteem will be good. If that is the case, then their self confidence will be good. If all three are present, then they will feel emotionally engaged in the learning scenario. And this optimises their brain for learning. This is because these four features provide the optimally rewarding environment. Reward stimulates dopamine secretion in the brain which is the main neurochemical involved in attention and learning.

At what age is the brain developed enough for logical thought, sequential learning, using metaphors and similes, independent learning, meta-cognition?

Read your Piaget. He got it right.

Does this change for males and females?

Social communication disorder is much more common in males than in females by a ratio of four or five to one. Therefore, all of the above is going to be most relevant to males in that they will be inclined to be emotionally immature compared to their chronological age—and this, of course, is normal. Another reason to encourage emotional literacy teaching in schools.

What is your view on single-sex education within a co-ed environment?

I don't think that one size fits all. Everyone is an individual. My only answer is test it and see. Some children will do better, some it will make no difference to, and some will do worse. I don't think we have the tools at present to predict which one is which. If you have both things available, then you can move a pupil in and out of the various environments. And, of course, ideally, every school should offer exactly this sort of flexibility. And it may be that pupils will do better in one subject in a single sex environment, and worse in others, and vice versa.

Does the gender of the teacher affect the learning?

I don't know the answer to this question. My instinct would be no, it is the personality that effects the learning.

How would you improve primary to secondary transition?

One school for all ages with gradual increase in the level of sophistication being offered and central emotional literacy training throughout the school from the moment the child enters reception.

If, like me you are a little rusty on your Piaget, I provide a brief summary below.

Definition

Jean Piaget (1896–1980) was a Swiss biologist and psychologist renowned for constructing a highly influential model of child development and learning. Piaget's theory is based on the idea that the developing child builds cognitive structures—mental 'maps' or schemes—to help them understand the environment around them. Piaget explained that a child's cognitive structure becomes more complex as they develop, moving from a few innate reflexes such as crying and sucking to highly complex mental activities.

Discussion

Piaget's theory identifies four developmental stages and the processes by which children progress through them. The four stages are:

1. *Sensorimotor stage (birth–2 years old)* The child, through physical interaction with his or her environment, builds a set of concepts about reality and how it works. This is the stage where a child does not know that physical objects remain in existence even when out of sight.
2. *Preoperational stage (ages 2–7)* The child is not yet able to conceptualize abstractly and needs concrete physical situations.
3. *Concrete operations (ages 7–11)* As physical experience accumulates, the child starts to conceptualize, creating logical structures that explain his or her physical experiences. Abstract problem solving is also possible at this stage. For example, arithmetic equations can be solved with numbers, not just with objects.
4. *Formal operations (beginning at ages 11–15)* By this point, the child's cognitive structures are like those of an adult and include conceptual reasoning.

Piaget outlined several principles for building cognitive structures. During all development stages, the child experiences his or her environment using whatever mental maps he or she has constructed so far. If the experience is a repeated one, it fits easily—or is assimilated—into the child's cognitive structure so that he or she maintains mental 'equilibrium'. If the experience is different or new, the child loses equilibrium, and alters his or her cognitive structure to accommodate the new conditions. In this way, the child erects more and more adequate cognitive structures.

This all presents a very interesting picture for our story. The development of the brain seems to be clearly understood, yet we appear to be ignoring that in our current arrangement of schooling. Brain development is clearly gradual, so we must try to develop our transition work to echo this. Like most things this is easier said than done. Secondary and primary see the world through different spectacles. So how do we bring this view together? Perhaps a good first step is to share spectacles!

Thinking back to the section on the one-room school, does that give us any pointers to the way forward? I asked Cindi for her view.

> A very significant aspect is the national questions that are arising about the division of grade levels into different schools. Such questions stem from lower achievement scores and higher dropout rates for students as they transition from one school to another—elementary to middle, middle to secondary, secondary to college. This is particularly evident in middle schools' test scores, dropout rates of students in their first year in secondary school, and likewise in the university setting. Would the trend reverse if students were not 'graduated' to another building with different leadership, culture, etc? Researchers touting data that suggest that private schools are being more successful than public schools often do not control for variables such as transitioning from school to school, consistency in academic expectations and culture, or other 'soft' variables. Some schools in the United States and the United Kingdom are creating pre schools through secondary school consolidated models that address these soft variables. These models will include all grades that operate as one school (often on a single campus), with one administrative leadership team that sets the expectations and culture, provides support for students via 'knowing' them and their academic, social and personal needs throughout their academic

careers, and provides well defined and articulated student learning outcomes that are achieved via backwards mapping techniques. These models are worth investigation.

As we move into the twenty first century, we in education must examine the 'new learners', the ones who can multi task in ways that other generations cannot even imagine, who have had computers as much a part of their lives as we had telephones and TVs, who view learning and schooling related to information access rather than a single book that must be memorized for future use, and who look at learning not as a finite body of knowledge needed to enter a job/career but things to learn or access when needed. Does the one room school model hold some secrets to unlocking the future of education? I believe so. If we reflect on the successes of the past and the needs of the future, considering how to develop cross walks, we will be stronger and better for the work. Professionally, we can see much further if we recognize that we stand on the shoulders of those who have gone before us. We must recognize that good teaching and successful and happy students who grow into productive citizens are not new concepts. The changes to which we must adjust are the societal ones. We can learn from the past, project the needs for the present and the future and build a stronger profession. By reflecting on the one room school educational model of the past we can unlock options for improving education for now and for the future.

At this point of the book, you could be excused for thinking the message is not a happy one. So far we have established that primary and secondary models are very different and don't work well together, that the needs of the individual are often not met and that the one-room school that we threw out had many redeeming features.

Fear not, please don't reach for the whisky bottle, all is not lost! The next section will help you analyse your own situation, and then decide what type of change is needed. The final section will then give you real examples of schools that are making a difference to the transition experience of their pupils.

Part 2

Part 2

How can alternative structures of schooling improve the situation?

Perhaps it is time to get radical—does changing the way we organise things actually help? In the section following this one we will look in detail at successful solutions (including our own at Serlby Park). However, reading about the work of others is rarely engaging unless you can connect it to your own situation.

Looking at education with an all-through perspective opens an exciting menu of partnership opportunities. Part 2 will help you analyse what changes might be possible in your own situation and then offer help and guidance on the different mechanisms for collaboration. This section will finish by outlining the latest theories of managing change, and describe how they can be used to provide the momentum necessary for successful transition.

Do we want to change our ways?

(to federate or not to federate!)

In this section I will start by helping you work out if you really do want to change and then Barry Bainbridge will give an outline of the variety of options that are available to you and explain how you begin the process. I will then look at a number of examples I have been involved in and use these to offer guidance.

Perhaps you should begin by answering some fundamental questions:

1. What are the most important educational skills a pupil should leave formal education with?
2. What are the most important life skills a pupil should leave formal education with?
3. What are the key attitudes a pupil should leave formal education with?
4. What are the essential qualifications for a pupil to leave formal education with?
5. Are you currently part of a system which delivers perfect solutions to 1–4?

(If 'yes'— stop now, pat yourself on the back, smile smugly, relax with a G&T and please, please e-mail me your information.)

6. Imagine you run a 3–18 through school. Zoe is 3 years old and has just been passed into your educational care—what are your hopes for Zoe when she leaves you aged 18?

(This should form the basis of your mission statement!)

7. Do you think the system you are in could be dramatically improved?

(If 'yes'—read on, you will find the next sections very useful; if 'no' close the book and use it to dig a head-sized hole in the sand!)

Hard, soft, chewy or all the way?

OK, so you have decided it is worth changing, you want to work closer with other schools—what are your options?

At this point I will hand the baton to Barry Bainbridge, who has more knowledge in this area than any other individual that I know of. Barry travels the length of the UK working with different groups who are on the journey of collaboration. He has kindly agreed to outline the possibilities that face you.

The range of all-through structures

None of the current regulations around collaboratives, federations, trusts or amalgamations were specifically written for all through structures, but they apply whether the planned combined structure is to be within phase or across the phases. The regulations are well established and there is full guidance available from the Department for Children, Schools and Families (DCSF), usually through the Trusts and Partnerships Division which will also provide further advice on request. The purpose of this section is not to revisit the regulations but to provide practical advice and examples of using the regulatory framework to establish a formal all through structure which will enable the school or groups of schools to look at education as a continuum to the benefit of the pupils. These structures are usually for pupils from age 3 to 18 but 3–16, 3–13 and 9–18 structures are also in existence or being discussed.

In many cases, good and even exceptional practice already exists between schools in different phases. Often because of proximity and always where there is a shared educational philosophy, small groups of schools across the country are working hard together to tackle the challenges of their communities by sharing expertise across the divisions in our system. For example, a primary school and secondary school sharing the same site in a disadvantaged northern city have collaborated so closely together that the new build will be a combined all through 3–16 school. However, in this school and in others like it, there is now a pressing need to formalise the relationship to ensure that the good work and collaboration are not lost should there be a change of leadership in either school.

Indeed, it is this need to formalise good practice and collaboration that provides the driving force behind many of the all through structures that are developing across the country. There are many instances where thriving schools can see the potential for pupils in working more closely together and, in these instances, the all through structure is driven by that shared philosophy. However, in some cases, it is the prospect of one of the partners retiring that has brought into stark relief the fragility of the relationship between the institutions. Similarly, the collaboration might be put under threat by promotion or even a significant change in the governing body.

Difficulties in recruiting headteachers are increasingly common in rural areas and urban estates alike, and this is providing another key 'driver' for groups of schools to come together in both horizontal and vertical structures. In some cases this is actively supported by local authorities both to provide leadership where there might not be any and to provide new forms of systems leadership which will bring an added dimension to the drive for continuous improvement. Devon is perhaps the best example of a proactive and supportive local authority in this context. It has produced excellent support materials and a federation protocol with practical guidance for schools wishing to federate, taking them through the process step by step. In rural areas, all through federations have the potential to sustain small remote schools, whilst at the same time providing sufficient size by grouping schools together to efficiently manage the system leadership requirements and to be an attractive option for talented leaders. In disadvantaged urban areas, all through structures can create a continuum of learning and support which can be a regeneration engine for the community.

Whatever the driver, once the need for a formal structure is identified the process of forming that structure can begin. There are a range of structures which can be considered but, firstly, it is essential that there is a clear vision of the desired educational outcomes for the children in the group of schools. How will the education of the children, the progress they make and their commitment to learning be enhanced by formally bringing the group of schools together? It is vital that the vision drives the structure and that everyone concerned with the process keeps this vision at the forefront of their thinking while they wrestle with the procedural and accountability issues which will inevitably arise. In potential all through structures, the educational benefits can be identified around the personalisation agenda and the establishment of an educational ethos and support mechanisms which will sustain the children throughout their schooling. The Consortium of All Through Schooling (CATS) has support materials which detail the potential additional benefits that all through structures can provide over and above the more usual phase federations.

The vision can be developed by a small group of senior staff from the group of schools which may potentially come together. In one real example, the headteachers of a primary and a sec ondary school had discussed the potential for an all through structure informally on a number of occasions. They brought together two members each of their senior teams with the chairs and vice chairs of governors from both schools for a full day workshop at a venue outside the schools. The workshop identified the key challenges in the community they served, the chal lenges in the schools and ways in which the service to the children could be improved further if they worked together from 3–16. The meeting was externally facilitated to ensure that they didn't stray into potential structural problems and, at the end of the day, they had a shared vision of the benefits for the children and the community at large which would keep later deliberations about leadership and management structures grounded in the core purpose.

In another real example, it was decided to launch the concept of a federation between a primary and secondary school in a presentation to about 200 staff and governors from the two schools, county council advisors and key players in the local community. An external expert was brought in to deliver the presentation and lead workshops and discussion sessions afterwards. The aim was to establish a general interest and enthusiasm for the idea of an all through federation and then facilitate workshops with interested staff and others to consider the structural implications.

Increasingly, schools are considering coming together in larger groups. The federation guid ance was revised in 2007 to increase the recommended maximum number of schools in a federation from five to nine and the Next Practice project for System Leadership, jointly run by the Innovation Unit and National College for School Leadership (NCSL), is currently developing exciting new structures ranging from a possible 'limited company' approach for a large group of schools in Wiltshire to a complete 'learning town', which will bring together all the schools in Winsford in Cheshire. Outside this project there are large 'soft' federations, such as Yeovil in Somerset where 23 schools are involved, and a potential learning town in Haverhill in Suffolk where up to 17 schools are exploring ways of working more closely together and formalising these arrangements.

Having established the vision for learning which will drive the formal structure, the next step is to consider what structures might be applicable to the partnership of schools. It is essential to bear in mind that the DCSF has moved away from imposing rigid structures and is developing a much more enabling role in which the structures are there to serve education and the regulations are broad enough to enable local groups of schools to develop a bespoke solution to meet their needs. This is an exciting prospect for innovative professionals and an opportunity to be grasped. Added to this is the Power to Innovate (PTI) which was enshrined in the 2002 Education Act. This enables schools to apply to have regulations suspended where a clear case can be made that, by doing so, the educational outcomes for children will be improved and that this improvement cannot be achieved in any other way. These are liberating times for talented professionals with clear vision and a drive to improve outcomes for children!

The more usual potential structures range from amalgamated schools through 'hard govern ance' federations, 'soft' federations, collaboratives and trusts. There are experiments with chari table companies and educational foundations, amongst others, but more time will be needed to assess their usefulness in the general context and they will not be discussed in this section. Trusts are also a case on their own and a great deal will be learnt from the 35 pilots currently being developed (they too will not be discussed in this section). However, it is worth noting that, as things stand at present, trusts are designed to be strategic bodies and would need underpinning federation structures to deliver joint appointments. Most of this section will be devoted to hard governance federations as they are by far the most common model.

Amalgamation

Amalgamation is the strongest model in terms of leadership and management of the combined institution and for governance. Lines of responsibility and accountability are clear and the leadership team can drive forward the vision for the new school. For example, at Serlby Park, a 3–18 Business and Enterprise Learning Community in a mining village in north Nottinghamshire, there is a strong leadership team with representation from the traditional phases in the system—the teaching and learning responsibility (TLR) structures embody the all through concept and it is clearly one school, deeply embedded in its community and with a strong vision for the value of education for the children it serves. Similar all through examples include Hinde House 3–16 School in Sheffield, the Hadley Learning Centre in Telford, and West London Academy.

The process of amalgamation is controlled by the local authority for the most part as it will involve the closure of at least one if not both (or all) of the existing schools to create the new entity. Strictly speaking, it is not an amalgamation at all but the creation of a new school. The local authority would control the consultation process for this to happen but recent changes in legislation now require a competition through which any interested party can make a proposal to run the new school, not just the local authority. In potential all through amalgamations, it would be possible to close one school and extend the age range of the other to cover the range of the closing school.

A potential pitfall for schools considering this way forward is the impact on the combined budgets of the two schools. In a federation, the schools concerned keep their separate legal identities and, therefore, their separate budgets. In an amalgamated school, it is one legal entity which will receive one budget driven by the local funding formula. Thus the new school will receive one allocation of funds for any non pupil weighted element of the formula. There are also implications for direct grants to schools from central government. Some of these difficulties can be overcome with the support of the local authority which might continue to fund the schools as if they were federated, or at least guaranteeing that there would be no loss of funding at school level, even if savings can be made at the centre.

Hard governance federations

A 'hard governance' federation is created when a group of schools come together under a single governing body. This is the most used structure in establishing federations of all shapes and sizes across the country. These federations have given rise to a variety of leadership structures which vary considerably in the range of accountability practices, physical structures and leadership roles. In creating a hard governance federation, the governors of the schools concerned control the consultation process, with the local authority being consulted along with other interested parties. Clearly, the enthusiastic support of the local authority would be welcomed by those seeking federation but there has been considerable variation in support from authority to authority. However, the recent leadership recruitment problems have encouraged a rethink in some areas as federation is increasingly being seen as a potential solution to these difficulties.

Once the vision described earlier has been established, the schools will need to develop a proc ess which will engage the key partners, provide answers to some of the structural and proce dural issues and include a statutory period of public consultation to enable the federation to be established. For the purposes of the illustration which follows, it is assumed that two schools, a primary and a secondary, are wishing to federate. The model works in other configurations equally well although the emphasis of some of the working groups might be different.

To begin the process, the two governing bodies will each need to resolve formally to explore the idea of a hard governance federation between the schools. They cannot resolve to federate at this stage, however enthusiastic they might be about the idea. Such a resolution can only hap pen after they have considered the outcomes of the statutory consultation. They should then each resolve to establish a joint committee which will explore the implications of the proposed federation. It is recommended that this committee would report back to extraordinary meet ings of the governors of both schools (these could be held together or separately according to circumstances) before going out to public consultation. This will ensure that key questions have been considered and agreed to present a coherent vision to the community. Finally, each gov erning body should agree the schedule of meetings and the timing of the statutory consultation process.

Ideally, the committee should not be too big to facilitate proper debate. One way forward would be to have five governors from each school: the chair of governors and four others represent ing the usual categories on the governing body, e.g. community governors, staff governors, et al. This committee could be further divided to look, perhaps, at leadership arrangements (the chairs), staffing and pedagogical issues (staff governors), potential parental concerns (parent governors), financial implications and models (local authority governors) and the potential impact on the community and neighbouring schools (community governors). There may well be other issues to consider but these are the most common. The headteachers should attend and advise the committee and sub committee meetings to ensure continuity.

External facilitation is extremely useful during this development stage as it allows the headteach ers to participate in the discussions whilst someone else runs the meetings and keeps everyone focused on the main task. If the committee meets to agree the consultation process between the two schools and the timetable for the whole process, each of the sub groups can then meet once to consider their issues and make recommendations. The committee can then meet again to receive these reports and prepare recommendations for the extraordinary meetings of both governing bodies. Once the issues have been resolved to the satisfaction of both governing bod ies, they can then go out to public consultation with some confidence.

In some cases, schools have been wary of the statutory consultation process and have seen it as potentially problematic. It is, however, a unique opportunity for engaging with the whole com munity and getting the vision for learning into every household. As long as everyone concerned understands how the vision will be achieved through federation, there should be nothing to fear. In some cases, potential federations have held an open meeting part way through the consulta tion process to encourage consultees to make their views known. This also serves to demon strate the openness of the process.

The period of statutory consultation must be a minimum of six weeks excluding any holiday peri ods. When the local authority is supportive, it can be useful to use their services as a more neu tral party to receive and collate any comments which come back from the consultation process. Where this isn't possible, the clerks to the governors may take on the role. The consultees must include the local authority, all staff at the schools concerned, all parents and the diocese, trustees, foundations governors and so on where relevant. It would be good practice to consult local professional associations, local community groups and churches, neighbouring schools and other groups which might have an interest, such as training providers, the Learning and Skills Council (LSC), the health authority and so on. The wider the consultation, the better to engage the community and influence the context within which the federation will work in the future.

The guidance for who must be consulted and the minimum that must be consulted on are contained in the guidance available from the Trusts and Partnerships Unit of the DCSF and are not produced here. However, as with the range of consultees, consider providing full details of the proposals and adding to the minimum (within reason) to ensure that this opportunity to get the message of the federation out into the community isn't lost.

Following the consultation period, the governors of both schools must meet together to consider any representations from the consultation. In many cases the representations have been so few and entirely positive that these meetings have been short. However, a good attendance by governors is essential to give credibility to the process. Since the date of this meeting will have been set at the beginning of the whole process, this should not present too many problems. Finally, both governing bodies need to meet to formally resolve on the federation. It is easiest if they both meet separately but in the same venue. The DCSF guidance suggests that this could be a neutral venue, ensuring that this is seen as the start of a partnership, not a take over. Assuming a positive outcome, the governors can then come together to mark the establishment of the federation.

The schools must then begin the process of forming the new governing body. The local authority must be informed and should help the schools to schedule a timetable for governor elections and appointments. Consideration must also be given at this point to governor support for the schools during this process, which can take between eight and 12 weeks. Ideally, this would have been done in advance during the consultation process. There are regulations for temporary governing bodies but the local authority should be able to advise schools on appropriate interim measures to deal with general matters and any disciplinary situations which might arise. A simple solution for most occasions might be for the chairs of governors to continue to take 'chair's action' for their respective schools until the new governing body can meet and elect the new chair. This would need the support of the local authority.

The process from the first meeting to agree the vision to the first meeting of the new governing body of the federation will usually take about six months. A recent federation in Herefordshire had its first meeting at half term in February and the federation was formally launched at the beginning of the autumn term in September. Things can take much longer but rarely will they happen more quickly than this. Having said that, it is not essential that the federation starts at the beginning of a new school year, or even at the beginning of a term, although most have chosen to do this.

Soft federations and collaboratives

The DCSF guidance describes two types of soft federations: a 'soft governance' federation which has delegated powers, and a 'soft federation' which has a similar joint committee to the soft governance federation but without delegated powers. The collaboration regulations are used to establish soft governance federations and for the purposes of this section, collaboratives will be treated as the same.

In practice the soft federation establishes a committee which can make recommendations to the individual governing bodies in the federation who then consider and authorise (or not) the recommendations. These are formal committees which meet regularly to consider key aspects of cooperation between schools. They can include joint working groups which develop policy and can have management appointments controlled by service level agreements (SLAs) and, occasionally, a central budget which each governing body has resolved to support. Such soft federations often deliver across large groups of schools and may include colleges of further education, but they also serve to illustrate the fragility of the collaborative structures discussed at the beginning of this section. Any significant change in school leadership or governance can destabilise the federation and more formal structures are increasingly preferred to give strategic and practical security.

Soft governance federations establish a committee which has delegated power. The decisions of this joint committee are binding on the participating governing bodies and this provides greater security for driving forward a vision for the federation and for appointments, although these would need to be underpinned by formal protocols and contracts. The joint committee might have budgetary powers in its sphere of delegation to facilitate rapid decisions on behalf of the group of schools. The SLAs and protocols which are developed to support the joint committee should include arrangements by which a school governing body can withdraw from the federation, along the lines of the formal requirements in the regulations.

These soft governance federations have proved to be very useful in delivering key aspects of the work of a group of schools, most particularly around the 14–19 agenda where schools are unable to deliver the full entitlement to pupils on their own. However, although they are statutory, they have similar fragility to that of the soft federation and if they are to assume a greater strategic role, there is a danger that the school governing bodies will be diminished. In some cases, soft governance federations are looking at alternative models, again mainly around the 14–19 agenda and the DCSF has responded to this by extending regulations to allow colleges of further education to participate in school collaboratives.

Conclusion

There is excellent guidance available from the DCSF on all aspects of federation and collaboration with some of the practical suggestions coming from the author's experience in establishing the first hard governance federation in the country. In addition, the Innovation Unit has a wealth of experience in this area and Devon County Council has been generous in making its excellent guides to federation available to others. For all through structures, CATS has an unsurpassed network of practitioners who have either been through the federation process or are in the process of doing so. CATS has also brought together expertise in the potential benefits of all through schooling and the development of innovative leadership and governance models. Contact details for each of the above can be found at the back of the book.

Not sure which is best for you?

If you are interested in forming a closer collaboration but are still not sure which type is appropriate then the next part is for you. First some light-hearted questions then some case studies.

1. **Why do we want to work more closely?**
   I don't know! = Stop now and find out before continuing

   Saves money/solves a buildings problem = Not a good reason for change—suggest you go away and think again

   Pupils will benefit from the change = Now you're talking—continue with the process

2. **Do we want to try something we could unpick if unsuccessful?**
   Yes = Now I could comment on your negativity, and assumptions of doom, but I won't. Perhaps your governors need the safety net? I suggest hard, chewy or soft, but not all through

   No = Keep an open mind—you could be a candidate for the all through option

3. **Do you want to keep separate heads for each school?**
   Yes = Any of the federated options may be up your street, but you will need to be serious about working together as a team—the autonomous head has no place in transition. Soft federation may be your easiest option

   No = Hard federation or even all through should be a real consideration

4. **Do you want to pool budgets?**
   Yes = Hard, chewy or all through all offer the ability to take a more flexible approach to matching budget to need

   No = You sound as if soft is your option! Maybe once you are federated the temptations of budget collaboration will entice you to something harder!

5. **Do you want to share governance?**
   Yes = Hard federation or all through hold the answer to your dreams!

   No = Soft or chewy for you. Chewy offers an excellent method for governing bodies to start bridge building

6. **Do you want to appoint some staff jointly?**
   Yes = Possible with any (but more complicated with soft and chewy)—an essential part of hard federation and the *raison d'être* for all through.

   No = You certainly aren't a candidate for all through, where it is not possible to do otherwise

7. **Do you want pupils to consider their education as a single progression?**
   Yes = Thank goodness for that—any of these solutions will help you on the journey!

   No = You can't be serious! I hope you haven't paid good money for this book! (I trust this is Cousin Jim's copy that has randomly opened on this page)

Sorting out why—some case studies (a transition agony aunt!)

At Serlby Park we are visited every week by a selection of guests from all over the country (and an increasing number of international ones). This long line of visitors has given an interesting insight into forming partnerships. For some of our guests the visit is their first step into any collaboration and the individuals sometimes show little knowledge of each other or any understanding of the reasons for any future partnership. For others the visit is a part of their own journey and the individuals show from their conversation the maturity of a strong relationship based on common principles. Each group brings with it a different perspective on partnership and in some way holds a mirror to our own. By responding to other's questions and listening to their reasons for the visit helps us to sharpen our own plans and strengthen our resolve to engage in major system redesign.

I believe that the selection of visitors can help me to provide some guidance to any reader who wishes to move their own partnerships or even wants to develop new ones. Recognising the delicate nature of relationships, and also respecting privacy, leads me to produce some case studies which I have anonymised. The relationships are all ones I have seen but the contexts and individuals are fictitious. I recommend you read each case study and then try to apply the lessons learnt to your own situation.

The groups I identify are:

a) 'Ask him, he's in charge'
b) 'We've brought everybody and his cousin'
c) 'We've been told to do it'
d) 'They are killing off our middle school!'
e) 'We've got a new building'
f) 'Trust in us'
g) 'It just makes sense'

a) 'Ask him, he's in charge'

Background
Based in a medium-sized town in the Midlands, the visitors are the headteacher of a 1,300 pupil 11–16 secondary, the chair of governors of the secondary and the headteacher of the largest (and most successful) primary school in the town.

Why did they say they were visiting?
The secondary head had heard me speak at a conference and wanted to take up the offer of a tour of Serlby Park that I frequently make (I even extend this proposal to you, dear reader!). He said that he had brought along his primary colleague because he wanted to explore taking control of their local agenda. He did not feel confident that his local authority had the ability or the inclination to provide an imaginative solution to schooling changes in their area. The chair of governors (a parent also prominent in community groups) was quick to explain that the secondary school was seen as the most successful in the area. She eulogised about the headteacher and proudly listed their achievements. She was happy to accompany and support the headteacher in any of his future plans. The primary head was noncommittal and just outlined how interested she was to see new ways of schooling.

What was the subtext of the visit?

The secondary head was very clearly the dominant partner of this visit, and also the relationship. He had organised the transport, paid for lunch and tried to control the conversation. The primary head gave hints that their personal relationship was not a strong one—it was professionally cordial, but currently there was no concept of a shared philosophy. Her body language showed a suspicion that there was a hidden agenda. Some unspoken questions echoed around the room: Why was only one primary head present? Was there any truth in the rumours of the secondary school going for foundation status? Would any resulting relationship be a true partnership or a takeover?

What collaboration is possible?

Without a closer personal relationship between the key players, any form of hard federation or amalgamation would be unadvisable. Formation of a soft federation would be a clear possibility, but some real care would be needed if it were to be successful.

What are the potential barriers to their success?

There is a strong possibility of any work being dominated by the secondary. It would be easy to imagine the secondary headteacher directing what the focus for the work would be and deciding how the primary school could benefit from them, rather than the opposite. The local authority could quickly become suspicious about the reasons for collaboration and there can be no doubt that other primary schools would view the work with suspicion. In a town of this size the balance of education should be a real priority, the other secondaries would possibly construe this work as an act of aggression.

What advice can be offered to this group?

There are some real issues that this group needs to solve before it moves down the road to collaboration: one is equality, or more precisely the lack of it. I start to worry when people give any suggestion that partnership is about imposing one mentality on another. As already discussed in the book, there are some real issues surrounding transition, and these alone provide an excellent drive to working together. However, looking at the problem from one perspective and then structuring the solution is almost guaranteed to miss the point, and will undoubtedly cause much upset along the way. If the group genuinely wishes for meaningful change then I can give them some clear next steps to follow their visit:

Short term:

1. On return, hold a meeting of all the feeder primary schools, outline the issues raised from your visit, highlighting the potential benefit for the young people of the area. Obtain a measure of the interest shown by primary schools. Ask for 'blue sky' thinking—think of possibilities without worrying about the problems.
2. Talk to the local authority and find out what their plans are for the area and in particular the other secondary schools. Is there the potential of an area-wide solution involving all phases of education?
3. Undergo research with young people in the area. What are their experiences of transition? What do they feel could be done to improve the situation?
4. Encourage the local authority to engage in an area-wide consultation of educational provision.
5. Arrange an informal meeting of all governing bodies in your potential collaboration (even those on the very fringes). Organise for an inspirational keynote speaker

41

(e.g. www.independentthinking.co.uk) to remind all parties of the important issues facing modern schools. Develop the common understanding that just leaving things as they are is not a realistic option.

Medium term:

6. Once you have plans in mind, make it clear that you are suggesting a genuine partnership. Set up committees and leadership groups that truly represent all those involved.
7. Ensure that the passion for the work outshines the practicalities and problems that will undoubtedly accompany it.
8. Form a pupil council to oversee the process from a student view point.

b) 'We've brought everybody and his cousin'

Background

The visiting group arrive in a small bus containing 35 people—they represent nursery, primary, secondary and further education in their area. The group consists of headteachers, class teachers, local authority officers, governors and councillors. They represent a medium-sized town in the South West of England. The town has decided to take a considered approach to the issues raised by an area-wide review which is to inform a major building programme under the government's Building Schools for the Future (BSF) strategy.

Why did they say they were visiting?

A couple of the key people in the group had been involved in the work of the Consortium of All-Through Schooling (CATS) and had proposed to their local authority that any solution should include an all-through option. The positive response to this proposal was to arrange the visit to a couple of areas heavily involved in collaborations between the phases, Serlby Park being one. The group wanted to know how we had been successful, what had driven the collaboration and any tips we could give them to move their ideas further.

What was the subtext of the visit?

On the face of it, the visit was an important step for the group, and a clear energy was evident amongst them. The fact that solutions were being considered that would disrupt the current organisational structure of education in the town was very positive. However, one did not have to scratch far below the surface veneer to find individuals' insecurities. When major change is proposed with benefit for the area, the individual must not be forgotten. Whilst many will express their delight in a modern enterprising solution for young people in the area, it is inevitable that the dominant questions in their own mind will be: How will my job change? Will I still have a job? How will my pay/prospects change? There was also a sub-text surrounding the question of who was in charge—was the person who arranged the visit (a secondary head) doing this because he wanted more power or was he genuinely just trying to encourage an area solution?

What collaboration is possible?

For this group the sky's the limit. In fact the group would probably benefit from the most imaginative solution possible. A soft federation or any loose association would probably untangle and could produce further tensions rather than solve them. To get a whole area to consider a solution is a great achievement and this may be the one chance for a radical solution. Clearly hard federation is a possibility, but with the potential of new buildings the opportunity for an all-through school, or maybe a hard federation of all-through schools, could help this town provide an education system that could become the envy of the world.

What are the potential barriers to their success?

One danger would be too much of the WIIFME (What's In It For Me?) attitude. Roy Leighton once told me that for any project to be successful there should be 30 per cent WIIFME—less than 30 per cent resulting in work that was unsustainable and more than this producing an ego-centric solution. Clearly with the number of headteachers and governors involved, the 'Who's got the biggest salary? Who's got the biggest office?' questions may come to the surface. One headteacher determined to keep their own autonomy could completely disrupt the process, introducing problems amongst the other partners as well as stirring up the local community. Often towns will contain very proud divisions, and a solution which does not acknowledge this runs the danger of developing severe community objection.

What advice can be offered to this group?

This project has the potential to produce outstanding results. The more organisations there are involved, the greater the potential for major success but also the greater potential for disagreement. To produce a successful community-wide solution it is vital that all parties are kept fully involved in the consultation. There should be opportunities for honest dialogue about possible personal concerns, but at all times a reflection back to the great potential for students of the area. My advice would be:

Short term:
1. Hold a joint training day event for every school in the area. At this event focus on the issues facing education in the UK and outline the concept that collaboration should be a major part of any solution. Enthusiasm must be a key part for any speaker and emphasis should be made on the career potential for anyone involved. It is also important to quell any fears about redundancy, making sure that the work is seen as a positive educational step rather than a cost-cutting exercise.
2. Encourage all groups to produce their own solution to this—encourage them to think out of the box and produce a range of collaboration ideas.
3. From the work emerging develop three alternative solutions—ensure none of the solutions is to 'leave things as they are'. Involve parents and pupils in amending the solutions and at all times keep up the positive attitude. This must be seen as something that is proactive and not reactive.
4. Encourage meaningful dialogue between all the educational staff in the town focusing on short current projects which will start to reduce the natural barriers between the institutions.
5. Produce an area-wide proposal document, outlining the reasons for the change, but also containing a clear timeline for the changes.

Medium term:

6. Pupils across all schools produce a magazine for circulation amongst the whole town.
7. Set-up a community board with representatives from governors, teachers, parents and pupils. Charge this group with leading the development into the next stage.

c) 'We've been told to do it'

Background

This group arrived in a mini-bus from an industrial northern city. They were a variety of staff and governors from a neighbouring primary and secondary school in the city. The visit had been arranged by the local authority who proposed to amalgamate the primary and secondary school into a one-site, new-build all-through school.

Why did they say they were visiting?

The local authority asked us to make a presentation to all those involved in the visit, and then subsequently to a group of influential councillors. They asked us to explain all the benefits of all-through schooling and to focus on how the academic achievement of pupils in the area can be enhanced. The visiting staff were keen to know how (and why) we decided to amalgamate. They openly expressed some scepticism about how suitable change would be in their area.

What was the subtext of the visit?

This was an unhappy group. The schools serve an area of considerable deprivation, which like many is also suffering from falling roles. The local authority felt that the best solution for schooling in the area was to develop a single school tailored for this particular community. The idea was a good one, but was floundering due to the way it had been handled. There was a lot of mistrust between the individuals on the visit—while walking around Serlby Park the group split into three distinct clusters: the primary, the secondary and the local authority. There were whispered comments and obvious negative body language shown by many. The fact that this was an imposed solution clearly angered the schools, and this was further complicated by some clear personality issues between the leaders of the two schools. A number of the visitors desperately wanted us to furnish them with reasons not to collaborate, rather than showing them the clear benefits.

What collaboration is possible?

On one hand, the proposed solution is by far the most preferable one. However, this has been so poorly introduced that strong negative views have already become entrenched. This really emphasises the importance of a collaborative process in the formation of any partnership. A soft federation would be one possibility with the hope that relationships would form and then closer links could develop. Other possibilities would be to try to hand back the control of the amalgamation to the schools or for the authority to dominate and make it clear that staff not excited by the process should move on.

What are the potential barriers to their success?

Where to begin on this one? Relationships, relationships, relationships! Without some major effort on rebuilding trust within this group there is no point in trying to form any type of partnership. To move out of your own comfort zone, considering new types of teaching to age groups you are unfamiliar with requires a huge personal commitment. To do this without the safety-net of others supporting you is unthinkable. Leaders sometimes fall into the mistake of seeing logical solutions, in the same way they would consider the next move on a chess board. Then having seen the solution they simply cause it to happen, forgetting that they are not dealing with chess pieces, but fallible, emotional, insecure human beings.

What advice can be offered to this group?
Sort it or stop would summarise my approach to this group! The need for considerable emotional intelligence in any form of collaboration is clear; when it is lacking the momentum for change is never established. When individuals in one school can moan about the other to complete strangers, this is a real indicator of potential failure. Presuming that stopping the process completely is not a possibility then my advice would be:

Short term:
1. Hold a joint staff meeting for all staff in the two schools. Have a national inspirational speaker clearly outline the issues faced by the UK student over the next 20 years. Develop the idea that change is desperately needed and that now is the opportune time to do it. Emphasise the potential benefit to the pupils and the staff, and outline the huge potential of a collaborative build.
2. Propose that there is initially little change to the way the school is led or managed. Build confidence that the good parts of each school will remain and possibly even flourish.
3. Develop subject-based teams across the whole age range, but avoid this being coordinated by the secondary head of department. Allocate a small amount of money to each group and challenge them to develop a project that will increase enthusiasm for their subject in both sections of the school.
4. Develop a small step approach to the developments between the schools. Avoid presenting grand visions; keep it to small engaging projects.

Medium term:
5. Create plenty of opportunities for relationships to develop between staff from the different schools.
6. Begin a series of one-day projects (as described in the Appendix B)—involve as many pupils as possible.
7. Set-up a series of staff socials (bowling, treasure hunts, etc).

d) 'They are killing off our middle school!'

Background
This group represented five schools from one of the few remaining areas which have a three-tier educational system (lower, middle and upper). The whole county has decided to disband the system and move in line with the more common national two-tier one. The area is preparing for its role in BSF and wants to ensure that the educational restructuring coincides with a major building programme. It has been decided that some areas might like to consider all-through models as part of their solution.

Why did they say they were visiting?
There was a general acceptance that the middle school system was disappearing, and once that was acknowledged then change was inevitable. To move from a three-tier solution to a two-tier one actually requires extreme change for the middle school. Staff have to choose in which phase they wish to work—a decision that may actually challenge their own ideologies. Some middle school teams of staff will have worked together for years and suddenly they, like their buildings, are torn apart. Faced with change of this magnitude it is easy to see the appeal of an all-through solution. A single school is trying to remove existing barriers and not develop a whole new one. In fact the reasons for initially developing middle school structures have many similarities with those behind all-through education. The group wanted us to provide them with evidence for the changes they wanted to propose. They felt in their hearts that one-tier education must work, but they wanted to see it in action. They were also keen to see how change could be made quickly and with the support of staff.

What was the subtext of the visit?
There were inevitable worries surrounding the imposed change from a three-tier system. Individuals were concerned for their own schools and for their own jobs. They feared that a drop in birth rate may require fewer places and therefore create an excess of teachers. They saw the single tier solution as a life-raft afloat in very stormy seas, and were desperate to cling to it. They took no persuading of the benefits of our work and were more interested in unpicking the procedures we used for joining our schools together. They were amongst our keenest guests gathering every scrap of information to feed to their local authority masters.

What collaboration is possible?
This group is ideally situated for the formation of a single all-through school. This could be done simply by closing all of the schools and extending the age range of one of them, then transferring all staff and pupils to the extended institution. Strangely, the models of hard and soft federation would probably be more difficult to arrange and potentially could have more drawbacks.

What are the potential barriers to their success?
The issue of falling rolls is one that could disrupt the process; if the local authority can see a surplus of places they are unlikely to agree to any solution which doesn't recognise this drop. It is vital to make sure the plans are realistic and are focused on pupils learning, and are not just a solution to save jobs. A further complication is brought about by the demographics and geography of the area. Whilst one of the middle schools sends virtually all of its pupils to the upper school, the other has about 50 per cent of its pupils heading towards a secondary in the neighbouring area. If both middle schools amalgamate (or federate) with the upper school represented in our group, where does this leave the neighbouring upper school? Whilst an all-through answer is an excellent solution to area restructuring, the complex relationships on the edges of any family of schools requires a very mature approach to networking, and vocal support and brokering from the local authority.

What advice can be offered to this group?
Although the group is obviously keen to be involved in major system change, their rationale for doing so may not always be pure. If this is to succeed, a major push on the

advantages to quality learning need to be emphasised. Just how will the all-through solution improve pupils' learning in the area? Some suitable next steps would be:

Short term:

1. Decide on a book which challenges the very basis of modern education, (e.g. *The Big Book of Independent Thinking* or *The Power of Diversity* by Barbara Prashnig or *The Learning Revolution* by Gordon Dryden). Buy a copy for every member of staff and governor.
2. Run joint training events where staff are encouraged to identify their top 10 issues raised by the chosen book. Form cross-institution groups and ask them to produce a common list and identify possible solutions (e.g. research shows that a majority of pupils learn better in subdued lighting—what implications does this have for any new school?).
3. Quickly involve staff from neighbouring areas in your 'challenging' discussions. Encourage everyone to see that collaboration is a perfect route to solving issues rather than causing them.

Medium term:

4. Look at ways of housing post-14 vocational provision on other sites—this has the advantages of allocating valuable space freed up by the falling roll, whilst also ensuring pupils from different phases will mix.
5. Focus on the Gifted and Talented pupils in your community. What innovative solutions can you find once you take away the barriers of having to move building at a particular age?
6. Begin production of a community newspaper. Involve staff and pupils in writing articles for this. Encourage the community to look on any structural change as solutions to a community problem.

e) 'We've got a new building'

Background
A group of five visited the school for a full day visit. An architect, a designer, an LEA officer and the designate headteachers of the primary and secondary sections of a new-build all-through school travelled from a market town in central England. The money has been secured for an exciting PFI build (no oxymoron intended!) to result in a 1,500 place all-age school. This group are the key people in moving the process along. The individuals arrive with many questions and an empty notebook.

Why did they say they were visiting?
The group wanted answers. They were on a tight deadline—the building was designed, foundations were started, the new school was to open in 18 months. They wanted to know how to do it, how to ensure success and what problems to avoid. They had read an article I had written for *ASCL* magazine and were keen to explore further the experiences I had outlined. They wanted to meet as many people as possible from across the full age range of the school. They were keen to see if the changes at Serlby Park were real or merely a figment of an overactive principal.

What was the subtext of the visit?
They were the victims of a well-meaning but simplistic local authority. The logic of the process so far could be summarised as:

- The schools in the area aren't working well together
- The government suggests all-though education might help transition
- Let's build a new all-through school
- Now let's appoint the heads
- Now let's appoint the rest of the staff put some pupils in.

This approach has resulted in the key players having only one thing in common—the building. No one was absolutely clear about what would happen inside it. The building is seen as the end of the journey, where in reality it is simply a container for its beginning.

What collaboration is possible?
The route is already decided for this group. They are to become the area's first all-through school. The entry at primary age will be simply one form, compared with a seven-form secondary cohort. The implications for this are that strong relationships must be built with existing primary schools in the area. It would be wise to consider a soft federation with the schools in order to ensure they felt part of the process and were immediately part of the new school structure. This would also enable the benefits of new resources to be shared with the community.

What are the potential barriers to their success?
This group have a problem that many would be envious of—they have a building. This shiny new monument to modern architecture sends out the wrong message. All-through education cannot be just bricks and mortar—it must be a philosophy. A rationale or common goal is one thing clearly absent from the group. Why are they doing this? At the moment the answer is simple: the reason for their visit is that they have to put something in the building. The group are hoping to take notes, copy what has gone well at Serlby Park and then apply it to their own building. This sadly is doomed to failure. The only thing they should be trying to copy from us is the process of discovering and clarifying their own philosophy. To approach the exercise as one akin to constructing an Airfix model is a potentially fatal error.

What advice can be offered to this group?
Great success is still within their grasp—they have some key ingredients, a supportive local authority, primary and secondary heads committed to all-through education and a modern building in which to house their work. This is akin to having all the dry ingredients for making a cake (useless without the liquid to bind it together); in their case, the binding agent is the passion and vision for their school. A measure of success will be if asked to describe their school three years from now, the buildings are not the first things on their list! These steps might help them on their way:

Short term:
1. Gather all staff appointed so far for a two-day residential. Before the meeting get everyone to use online leadership style analysis tools (Roy Leighton has some great examples). Begin your work together by comparing and contrasting the results of

your leadership analysis. Encourage the group to look at the balance of the team and celebrate their diversity rather than alienating someone who has an unusual profile.

2. Focus on a picture of some 3 year olds from your community. As a group, produce an outline of your wishes for these pupils when they leave your school 15 years from now. What do you hope your school will have given to them? This is the basis of your mission statement—what is your school actually about?

3. Give each person a cross-phase responsibility (if you restrict yourself to your current area of expertise you will be setting out completely the wrong blueprint for your school). Then ask each person to produce an action plan outlining the key developments they see as: essential, before opening, in the first five years, and then in the next five years. Possible areas of responsibility could include personal development, core skills, independent thinking, enterprise or study skills.

4. Ask each person to imagine the school has been open for five years. Their job is to take a VIP guest around the imaginary school, focusing particularly on their particular responsibility. Describe what can be seen and what has been occurring.

Medium term:

5. Now it is time to begin formalising your plans. Produce a document for parents and the community outlining your plans for the new school. Hold consultation meetings where parents and pupils have the opportunity to refine the plans themselves.

6. Ensure all new staff appointed are applying to be part of the vision and not the building.

7. Make sure that all structures in the school echo your core philosophy. Don't do anything just because this is the way it has always been done. Remind yourself of the work of Margaret Wheatley (see later in this section): organisations should be built on a set of common principles not on an exhaustive set of rules!

It would be easy for this group to assume that it did not have time to indulge in the above 'frivolities'. In fact, there is never a situation where change should be planned without clear understanding of why that change is occurring.

f) 'Trust in us'

Background

This group were quite unusual. They represent a deprived area in an industrial city in the North West of England. They have been working on producing a 'one-stop shop' for all the services required by the community. The group consists of local employers, local authority, community groups, special schools, primary and secondary schools, social workers, health professionals and representatives from higher education. The group is proud that it has been working together on this project for over a decade. They have a building programme already underway and the new site will open in about one year. Initially they asked me to support their work in their own area and then representatives visited Serlby Park.

Why did they say they were visiting?

The group have a building already underway. They have long established community support and a trust board who meet regularly to plan the development of the site. There is a general belief that putting all facilities in one place will support the community, but there are still some question marks over how integrated the schooling can/should be.

The group want evidence that all-through schooling works and guidance on how to ensure that it does.

What was the subtext of the visit?
The group have a very interesting but complex structure. In theory the special school headteacher has been given the role of project management, but the reality is that the real power base is the university who are keen to 'badge' this as their project. The group have been meeting for many years, but rather than producing a tight-knit team clearly focused on one goal, it seems to have produced a number of sub-groups with very entrenched views. I was somewhat alarmed to discover that the primary and secondary school were hardly on speaking terms and that the separate parts of the building had been finalised without joint discussions. A number of very passionate and able people make up this trust, but they currently appear to be pulling against each other rather than collaborating.

What collaboration is possible?
The formation of a trust may actually have clouded the issue for this group. They are already engaging in a process of forming federations on the journey to eventually becoming an all-through school. In many ways this is a logical route, but has the danger of becoming swamped in bureaucracy. A further solution would be to disband all current formal structures and move straight to the formation of a new single all-through school. The new organisation would have the advantage of being able to carve its own path and hopefully reduce some of the evident internal politics.

What are the potential barriers to their success?
Anything that takes over a decade in the planning runs the danger of losing focus. Without a small group or a key leader driving this type of development it will drift. To approach moving into a shared building with the key phases of education having little or no relationship is like building a brick wall without cement—one sneeze and the whole thing will fall apart! Whilst I would recommend doing any project to gain as wide a community support as possible, this group faces another danger. There is real potential that the external groups dictate progress and that the new educational relationships which should be at the core of the development become an afterthought. Personal relationships between staff of the different phases are desperately needed. Co-location will inevitably bring many practical issues and tensions—if the separate schools which make up this project retain their current segregation the gap between the phases will widen.

What advice can be offered to this group?
A very careful balancing act is required: educational direction needs to be regained but without losing valuable community backing. One possible way of doing this would be:

Short term:
1. Appoint a permanent (hopefully inspirational) leader for this project. This person should be given the role of leading the move into the buildings but also taking control of the whole project for at least the first two years of operation.
2. Arrange a joint meeting between all the school staff involved in the project. Enthuse about the benefits of the collaboration for the pupils of the area. Outline the benefits seen in other all-through environments (see Part 3), and highlight the clear potential for professional advancement for any staff involved.

3. Begin some immediate cross-phase projects, making sure to follow the guidance in Part 3 (don't let initial work focus on standards!).

4. Allocate the community groups with some important but non-educational tasks. For example, this group would be ideal for focusing the conversation about naming the new one-stop shop and for deciding on a uniform policy. Devolving real leadership to smaller groups will empower them and also relieve some of the larger political tensions.

5. Urgently call a meeting with the designers/builders and find out what still has the ability to be changed in the plans. Where some flexibility is still possible, find out the latest date that decisions can be made. Encourage a wide variety of the staff in all institutions to become involved in the decisions about colours and movements within the building. Ensure that the question, 'Will the building help us to improve transition?' is asked at every turn.

Medium term:

6. Set up smaller sub-groups of the trust, ensuring staff representation from each school. Devolve power to these groups for particular areas of responsibility and ask them to devise an action plan for their area.

7. Form a student committee with representatives from each phase. Ask the committee to produce a student guide to some Frequently Asked Questions.

8. Develop a series of staff and pupil socials aiming to get as full an involvement as possible.

9. At every possible moment inject a sense of fun and passion. Without enthusiasm this project will not reach its potential!

g) 'It just makes sense'

Background

This group of three headteachers are from a small town in the Midlands. They represent an infant, junior and secondary school whose grounds are all adjacent in a pleasant edge of town location. Each headteacher has been in their job for at least five years and they have already had a number of joint training days, with a variety of projects arising from these. They describe some excellent transition activities, but are quick to acknowledge that they are far from solving this thorny issue.

Why did they say they were visiting?

The group are much more comfortable in each other's company than many other visitors. They explain that they want to strengthen their relationship and see the logic of moving to some type of single institution. They hope to gain evidence to take to their local authority which (like many others) is nervous about change and slow to support those who show initiative. They also hoped to gain further ideas for effective transition and to back up their own theories about the benefits of all-through education.

What was the subtext of the visit?

This is one of the most straightforward of groups—to a certain extent, what you see is what you get. However, there was an unspoken sense of trying to look after their own area of town. The whole area was having a review in light of shifts in demographics and, with a fall in birth rate, there were some rumours about possible closure of one or more schools in the town. This all-through solution would secure the long-term survival of all three schools. Another issue which has not yet been solved by these three is how the new 'institution' will be led. It appears that the secondary head assumes that he will naturally be the overall head of the organisation; it is unclear if this view is completely backed by the other two!

What collaboration is possible?
The full range of collaboration is open to this group: soft federation, hard federation, all-through school and anything in-between. The three heads themselves seem to prefer the single all-through school option; however, they have major concerns about the support of the LEA for this option, particularly as the financing is more complex for this than for hard federation.

What are the potential barriers to their success?
Clearly this group needs to force its local authority to be honest about its intentions. It is always advisable to request such information in writing as changes in personnel at the LA can lead to later issues. Another big issue for them is to introduce some real clarity into their own relationship: what does each want out of the collaboration? The lack of open agreement about the best way to lead the resulting partnership could grow to become a severe issue. Even strong relationships will be strained during such times of major change and it is vital that the staff of each school see only cohesion between the three of them.

What advice can be offered to this group?
This group deserve to succeed. They have built a strong relationship based on improving the transition experience for pupils, and have the passion and drive required for success. My advice to them would include:

Short term:
1. Bring the key officers from the local authority on a fact-finding trip to Serlby Park (or suitable alternative). Come armed with questions and ask them of Serlby Park and of the officers.
2. Follow up the visit with a letter to the director for education and social services requesting confirmation of any statements made during the visit.
3. Each headteacher to produce their own version of the perfect leadership structure for the new collaboration. This should be shared with the other two at a meeting (allow at least half a day for this process!). Attempt to combine/eliminate versions until a single structure evolves.
4. Use an external consultant to chair a meeting where each of the groups' strengths and weaknesses are discussed. Match the personality profiles with the leadership structure produced in (3). Consider if there are any obvious gaps and who might fill these. Discuss who will be the named leader for the organisation and set the parameters for this role, clarifying the expectations for the style of leadership to be used.

Medium term:
5. Involve as many staff as possible from the three schools in the planning. Spread the enthusiasm, generate the passion and paint a picture of what could be achieved.
6. Begin amalgamating as much of the support structure as possible. For example, if one cook supervisor retires look to joining teams together and providing a unified catering

service. Other areas very appropriate for this type of change include caretaking, special educational needs support, grounds maintenance, health and safety, and ICT support.

7. Ask the student council from each school to gather questions from their own pupils regarding their worries and hopes for the new amalgamation. Then representatives from each group should present responses in a series of assemblies.

8. Involve staff and pupils from all schools in the production of a mural to grace the entrance of the new school.

Do you want to lead change?

Assuming you are still with us, we are now getting to the heavy stuff—making change happen. For this to occur you need to be prepared to be challenged in everything you do. For me the challenge originated from the incredible Roy Leighton. Here he characteristically questions the very foundations of your educational being.

The conditions for growth in the organic organization by Roy Leighton

Nowhere will our children's capacity to survive in the twenty first century be more tested than in the numerous 'organisations' that they will, by necessity, have to have at least a passing engagement with.

Look around your own organization and ask yourself, 'Would I want my children to work here?' If the answer is 'yes' then you are indeed a fortunate individual and probably self employed or a member of the senior leadership team.

If the answer is 'no' then what is it about the organization that makes you want to run for cover? Is it the tedious red tape and bureaucracy? Almost certainly, but that is not the main thing. What about the working conditions and finances? Well, these can always be improved and it is the way of men (and women) to want more and better.

So what is it that we fear will harm, block or in some way damage the fruit of our loins? It is the other adults. The so called colleagues who, for a million and one reasons, will seek to upset, intimidate, bully, belittle or in some way bugger up the confidence, vision and energy of our babies. When someone gets past a certain age (and that age will vary from person to person) they believe, for reasons better known to themselves, they are now an adult. Adult. Grown up. Capable of existing alongside others in a productive and mature way.

The trigger for this flimsy assumption might be a qualification (degrees are always a dangerous ritual that lead people to believe they have now joined a grown up world). What about money? Even worse than qualifications is cash. How many cash rich but personality and sensitivity barren individuals have you met? Oh, I am not knocking wealth creation. That would be veering towards naivety which is the close relative of immaturity. It's just that cash without character makes me want to reach for the off switch.

Letters after your name and money in the bank can give rise to the illusion that we are something that we may not be. However, in my experience, more than both of these, the mirage of maturity that so seduces individuals to drink at the parched, sandy bank of nothingness is management. It is here that we see people leap into massive assumptions about their own gifts and talents. This is partly from misguided expectation but mainly from access to the tribe that is the senior leadership team—the SLT.

In schools where I have worked I have advised that they abolish the SLT. Not the people (although in some cases that has been exactly what they needed to do). No, the name, the title, badge, office. Call it what you will. Let us quickly look at this word by word:

Senior—we are older and/or wiser than you so just get on and do it!

Leadership—we lead, you follow. Do not question. Yours is not to reason why…

54

Team—Howls of derisory laughter. If your understanding of creating a 'team' is a weekend away in some posh hotel with an overpaid consultant who assists you in 'bonding' and 'sharing a vision for all', and then you come back and bitch about other members of the team, you are not only missing the point, you probably never saw it.

So, the task that lies ahead for all our children is dealing with the kids that think they are grown ups. For that to happen they need to have developed not only a language of learning but also a language of what maturity looks like. Fortunately, thanks to the extraordinary life and work of Dr Clare W. Graves, we now have this in his model of emergent adult evolution. The block to apply ing this reasonable, intelligent, practical and insightful model is that we have to take it off the page and put it to work. And this is the gap that only adults can breach. Do we know but do we not do? Any organisation that wants to take the vision statement and make it real requires continu ous renewal, reflection and risk.

If you or your organisation has a vision statement but the childish behaviour of you and your col leagues is preventing anything other than talk to take place, you do not have a vision, you have an illusion. The way to turn the illusion into reality is to wake up. Better still, grow up.

Roy likes to provoke and would be upset if you were not at least slightly uneasy about parts of his section. The key part is how you respond to Roy's challenge. If you are ready for some major change here are some ideas to help you.

How can I persuade others that change is needed?

Creating the environment for change

'But everyone says what a great job we are doing—
now's the wrong time for change!'

The above cry can be heard across this fair land whenever something new is suggested, and when the idea is radical the call is loud and clear. No successful organisation is keen to embark on change, but schools approach the top of the 'resistance to change' list. The reason for this is clear to anyone who has led a UK school—success is fickle, often judged in isolation on league tables without all the necessary information. The road to perceived accomplishment is a rocky one and staff, parents and governors will loudly proclaim, 'We are successful because of the way things have been done for the past five years, therefore we must continue doing the same forever.' OK, they might not use quite so many words, but the message will be the same.

General Eric Shinseki, retired US Army Chief of Staff, challenged, 'If you don't like change, you're going to like irrelevance even less!'

Of course anyone trying to resist all change is missing a basic rule about life, which I often paraphrase as, 'The one thing you can be sure about the future is that you can be sure of nothing.' This is explained with some clarity by the business guru Charles Handy in *The Empty Raincoat*, a book written for all organisations to help them plan for a successful future. In it he develops the concept of the sigmoid curve.

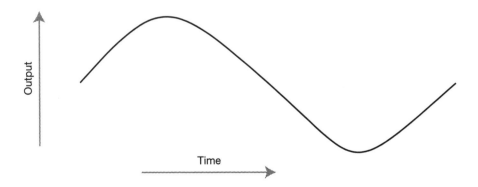

He has observed that all organisations (business, governments, sports teams and schools) undergo a sigmoid curve. The Y axis (the 'up' one for the less mathematical amongst us) is a measure of output. This can be financial profit, productivity, examination success or any other appropriate indicator. The X axis is a time span appropriate to each situation. Whilst the exact units change, the clarity of the sigmoid curve is quite astounding. In simple terms it is clear that any successful venture will inevitably face a downturn in its success. The length of time between curves is variable but Handy observes that the time span appears to be lessening over the past 20 years and is usually a matter of a few years, or in some cases even months. It is usually easier for an external eye to identify an organisation's position on a cycle, but it is an interesting activity to carry out at the next meeting of your leadership team—see if you can agree where you are on your sigmoid curve. You will quite likely find yourself closer to the peak than feels comfortable.

The bad news is that most organisations do not realise they have passed the peak of their curve until they are well on the downward slope (point A on the diagram below); sadly by then many factors will be conspiring to make it unlikely that the full dip can be avoided.

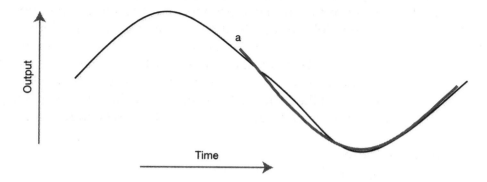

The good news, however, is that if change can be made before the peak at point B in the diagram below, a second sigmoid curve can be started causing a raising of potential.

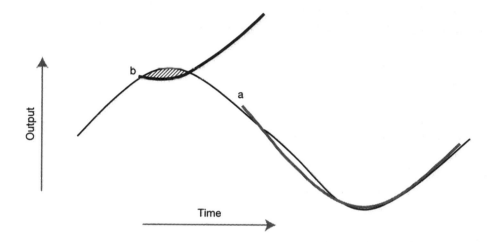

This phenomenon can be seen in any long-term successful company—even before the peak of its success is reached new and innovative ideas are being developed. Now the sharp witted amongst you (which I suspect must be the majority of you) will have spotted the dilemma—it is akin to being told that the best time to eat a great cheese is about seven days before it goes off; in other words by the time you realise, it's too late! The solution is therefore to always assume the next peak is imminent and to begin change. This alertness towards change avoids complacency and best fits a school to meet the new challenges of the twenty-first century.

So if Handy is correct and the timescales for curves are getting shorter, the implications for all organisations must be to constantly anticipate change. Does it matter if you anticipate a downward turn that doesn't occur?

The hatched area on the graph indicates the area of change—during this interim period the previous curve and new curve coexist. As long as an organisation remains alert during this time it is not too late to abandon or modify any changes that have begun. Schools are an ideal place to maintain the change momentum, as long as new ways of leading are introduced.

Is now the time for system redesign?

Professor David H. Hargreaves (prolific educational author for more than 30 years and now Associate Director at the Specialist Schools and Academies Trust (SSAT) and Emeritus Fellow of Wolfson College, Cambridge) has recently chosen Serlby Park as one of his 10 System Redesign schools. In *System Redesign: The Road to Transformation in Education* (2007), he identifies 20 reconfigurations which he believes are essential if schooling is to respond to the demands of the twenty-first century. At Serlby Park we are actively developing at least 17 of the 20. It is interesting to note that Professor Hargreaves chooses areas central to all-through education as his first three reconfigurations.

Institutional reconfigurations (10)
1. From single to multiple institutions
2. Merging of phases—primary/secondary/special/further/higher
3. Flexible and permeable age cohorts
4. School day, term and year
5. Flexible time schedules
6. Design of buildings and learning spaces
7. Competence-based, transdisciplinary curriculum
8. Academic/pastoral division
9. Smaller units within schools
10. School and workplace

Role reconfigurations (5)
11. Co-construction between stakeholders
12. Governance
13. Widespread, school-based innovation
14. Initial teacher training and continuing professional development
15. Partners as teachers

Leadership reconfigurations (5)
16. Flatter, less hierarchical staff structures
17. Distributed leadership
18. Student leadership
19. Leadership development and succession
20. Decision-making methods

Professor David Hargreaves is currently one of the most influential figures in education, and with his influence through SSAT, we must be hopeful that genuine system change is just around the corner. It seems likely that when this reconfiguration arrives improved transition will be one of the first benefits.

How can new ways of leading support change?

If an old fashioned hierarchical model of leadership is being adopted, the school will not be flexible enough to change—everyone waits for their instruction from on high—even if that person is sharp witted and forward thinking, delays are inevitable.

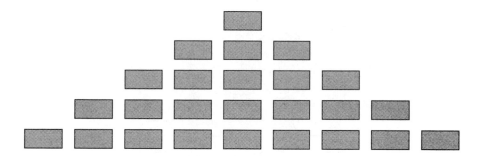

Hierarchical models are comforting to the system leader; they fill the predefined shape of the organisation perfectly. In a stable and completely predictable world they make perfect sense. If a school had identical pupils with clearly defined needs, required for a specific and unchanging future, why would anyone need to do anything different year from year? If a member of the leadership team leaves the above model their replacement is clear: replace one box with another perfectly identical box. Written like this we can all see the narrowness of this type of thinking, yet many schools continue to hang on to 'the way things have always been done' like the shipwrecked cling to the flotsam.

Handy encourages us to consider modern jobs as inverted doughnuts.

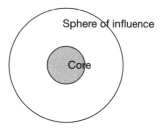

The centre is the core or defined role, the next circle is that role's sphere of influence. In this way the individual is no longer a 'slave to the system' but has the ability to help shift the whole organisation. I prefer to think of the role as an amoeba, with the core as the nucleus and the less regular, more flowing cell walls being the area of influence. This type of role is considerably more fulfilling than a traditional one where the individual is completing a number of predetermined tasks. It is, however, particularly stressful for any individual who does not fully understand this new type of role. To be given the role, and believe you have to fulfil even more, is to miss the empowerment it gives you.

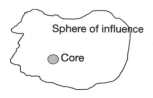

When a whole team is considered in this way, the adaptability of the organisation becomes clear. Overlap between roles is no longer something to be avoided at all costs, but instead is a desirable strengthening of the overall structure. When one member of this dynamic leadership structure is underperforming or leaves, their position can be covered by others without major concern. The system can adapt to the strengths of a new recruit rather than trying to make them fit their predecessor's shoes.

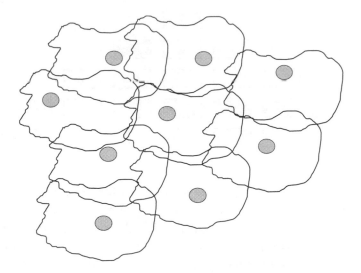

A school with this type of structure is much less dependent on the individual—this is not a 'heroic head' model. Anyone towards the centre of the model is able to ensure that the school adapts to issues on a daily basis. This type of leadership requires courage and belief, which many find more challenging than the traditional model; responsibility falls on many more shoulders, but so do the rewards.

Organic organisations

In her thought-provoking book, *Leadership and the New Science – Discovering Order in a Chaotic World*, Margaret Wheatley argues that organisations should be considered as living things, governed by the same basic laws of science as the rest of the world.

She points out that natural processes aren't locked rigidly into one physical form, and asks what streams can teach us about organisations:

> "The stream has an impressive ability to adapt to change, to let power shift to create new structures but behind the adaptability, making it all happen, is the water's need to flow.
>
> Organisations lack this kind of faith, faith that they can accomplish their purposes in varied ways and they do their best when they focus on intent and vision, letting forms emerge and disappear."

Most schools still adopt the manufacturing style of leadership where micromanagement is the order of the day—everyone is told what to do when. When allowed to flow, an organisation's exact path is unplanned—but the general progress is!

"To live in a quantum world to weave here and there with ease and grace we need to change what we do, we need fewer descriptions of tasks and instead learn how to facilitate process. We need to become savvy about how to foster relationships, how to nurture growth and development. All of us need to become better at listening, conversing, respecting one another's uniqueness because these are essential for strong relationships."

Her work has been fundamental in the development of Serlby Park (see the end of Part 3). She encourages organisations to avoid trying to precisely design their whole structure—she points out that once you realise that an organisation is living (almost like a plant), when you place a box around it its growth becomes restricted and the most you will ever achieve is to fill the box. Wheatley likens successful organisations to fractals. If your mathematics is rusty, fractals are large structures made from the repeating of smaller units or mathematical relationships and occur naturally—for example, the fern below, where the smallest structure is a perfect miniature of the whole plant.

If this is the first time you have witnessed this phenomenon, study the smallest floret of cauliflower under a hand lens where you will observe another example of this natural magic. As Margaret Wheatley eloquently describes:

"I believe that fractals have direct application for how we understand organisations. All organisations are fractal in nature, I can't think of any organisation that isn't deeply patterned with self similar behaviours evident everywhere. I am often struck by the similar behaviour exhibited by people in an organisation whether I am meeting with a factory floor employee or a senior executive.

Self similarity is achieved not through compliance to an exhaustive set of standards and rules, but from a few simple principles that everyone is accountable for, operating in a condition of individual freedom."

The message is clear for the innovative learning community: ensure the principles, the relationships, the respect are developed and let the structure grow as a fractal from this basis. If these core factors are correct, incredible complex structures can grow; on the other hand, if personal relationships are poor and mistrust abounds no successful organisation will result.

Ready to start growing your new organisation?

Read on!

Part 3

Part 3

What can you do about it?

Some examples of solutions found by schools in similar situations to your own

Having read the last section I hope you have some ideas of ways you can develop your partnerships between the phases. You will probably be looking for some first steps, trying to find some win-win examples to gain people's confidence. To me it is clear that our differences are so great that direct formal contact between primary and secondary schools could be counterproductive—focusing on the differences rather than building the relationships from which transition could grow.

It is like the meeting of two railway companies, both working on different rail tracks, but wishing to transfer between lines.

If the meeting focuses purely on the track width—one side (and size) will win, one will lose—it is unlikely relationships will develop, and any future dispute will almost certainly not be resolved. What is needed is a series of events where the future of rail travel is investigated and a long-term solution developed.

The same is true for education—it is important that meetings do not just focus on the validity of SAT levels between the phases. Any meeting set up to discover 'Is a primary level 5 the same as a secondary one?' is doomed to failure. Disagreement and entrenchment will certainly follow, therefore meetings and projects should be in a neutral ground where new approaches can be developed unhindered.

I became aware of the minefield surrounding liaison meetings in Hull, when in the1990s as Head of Science I was instructed to form better relationships with the feeder primary schools. An evening was set aside for all subject areas to meet with appropriate staff from the primaries. (It is not difficult to work out that this approach was instigated by the secondary—such a subject-focused series of events immediately alienates the smaller primaries who often have individual teachers overseeing more than one subject at a time). Those that were able to attend were guests of the secondary from where the agenda and meeting were controlled.

The initial meeting was far from successful, with attempts to map the curriculum immediately falling on problems; the secondary logic that everyone should agree on a common way of teaching the subject cuts across the primaries' individuality. Primaries have developed their themes and projects to support learning in a way that maximises their own staff and resources, and are understandably unwilling to march to a single tune—particularly that of the secondary. The position becomes even more complicated when most primary schools 'feed' more than one secondary, so the concept of producing a single curriculum could only possibly work if *all* schools delivered *all* subjects in a set way at a set time—the kind of 'sausage machine' mentality long since abandoned, and completely at odds with the government's push on personalisation!

So what to do? Clearly a common approach to subject content, pedagogy and levels must benefit pupils and result in a smoother transition, but to assume this common approach is actually that of the secondary is the biggest barrier to finding a solution.

The only long-term answer to the problem must be to build relationships. When e-mails, telephone calls and 'pop-in' visits are common-place, trust will develop. Once trust is evident, new ways of working will naturally develop. Although government will often have us believe that the quickest way from A to B is always a straight line, this is clearly not the case if long-term change is required.

The most important way to begin any building is to check your foundations—what do you *all* want from the project? (Don't assume your wishes are everyone else's!) Things that people around the table will have assumed as educational facts may not actually be true.

We all accept that our minds can be fooled—look at the following series of pictures as proof:

How many people can you see?

Now swap the top
two quarters
of the picture over.

Resulting in this.
(Check it if you don't
believe me.)

How many people do
you see now?

So if you can't trust your own eyes, are you quite so convinced that you know everything about the educational issues you face? I thought not!

Why not start your transition meeting in a different way?

Six steps to a successful transition meeting

1. Warm up with an educational 'thunk' (see www.independentthinking.co.uk by Ian Gilbert, e.g. 'Is a library with no books still a library?')
2. Ask everyone to share one thing they are very proud of from last year's transition.
3. Ask everyone to share one concern about transition.
4. Ask each secondary teacher to voice one thing they don't understand about the primary phase.
5. Ask each primary teacher to voice one thing they don't understand about the secondary phase.
6. Ask for suggestions on a special event that could be delivered as a team.

By agreeing on a common event (see some suggestions that follow), future meetings have a non-phase specific focus with joint ownership—all evidence suggests that the increased understanding and trust results in a far stronger liaison about the minutiae of the curriculum.

This section of the book contains practical ideas for things that have actually worked in transition. I have split them into three parts:

a) **How can I start improving relationships?** One-off activities, ideal for short sessions. These are ideal as first events or as part of a longer transition programme.
b) **How do we build strong foundations for transition?** Curriculum-based projects. These are examples of longer projects that have focused in one or more areas of the curriculum. They are often a product of great personal commitment by a few individuals who build very strong working relationships.
c) **How do we build new ways of learning?** Whole school projects. Examples of how common approaches between schools can grow to affect all aspects of transition. This section is for those who are really serious about making a long-term difference.

The examples and case studies described all show ways that have proved successful in a particular school with a particular context. The aim is to set out a smörgåsbord of possible techniques and methods of approach. As you browse through the exotically presented dishes, from a variety of inventive practitioners, remember that any (or all) of these could work for you, but the key ingredient for each one is the developing of long-term strong and trusting relationships.

How can we start improving relationships?

The first step is always the most difficult! In Appendix C I have included 20 ideas from many sources. They are all activities which could be carried out in a few hours. They are 'another brick in the wall' of transition. Many of the activities could (and do) occur within individual schools, but have been developed to be effective across a range of age groups. The crosses on the age chart simply show where they have been used—most of them could be adapted for almost any combination of years. Where support materials are available the website location of the resources is listed.

> "Take the first step in faith. You do not have to see the whole staircase. Just take the first step"
>
> Martin Luther King

Take your first step— go to Appendix C!

I recommend that you use the examples in Appendix C as starting points for your thoughts, not as ready-made solutions. Indeed, feel free to change them in any way, and contact me if you discover any new activities. Additional ideas and materials to support the activities are available free of charge at www.droppingthebaton.com. Whatever you do, concentrate on forming relationships between the schools—each partnership between teachers of different phases is likely to produce benefits over a long time. Take for example the Air Fair project I worked on when in the 1990s I taught at Archbishop Thurstan School in Hull.

Air Fair

This was the result of the experiences from the first cross-phase meeting at Archbishop Thurstan School. It was agreed that rather than focus on curriculum smoothing we would instead develop a science day to celebrate the work completed in the subject across the whole age range. In one move the transition work was now rewarding as opposed to critical. A number of meetings were held to answer the key questions:

- *What should be the theme*? It was decided that the topic of air was relevant and could be addressed from each key stage.
- *Where should it be held?* The local community centre to avoid association with any one school and to encourage access by parents.
- *What format should it take*? It was felt that a fete would be the most suitable format, allowing pupils of all ages to run stalls and for side-shows/demonstrations to be included by local businesses.
- *What record would be kept of the day?* It was agreed that a team of young journalists from across the age groups would produce a newspaper celebrating the event.

This format allowed for work to continue in individual schools, without a great amount of central direction, and allowed for schools to play to their own strengths and not feel marginalised by a lack of expertise or equipment. Local and national industries were surprisingly keen to be involved, happy to be addressing all phases of education in one fell swoop.

Activities included:

- Working with helium (demonstrations using balloons)
- Using parachutes (comparing shapes, materials and holes)
- What happens when air gets very cold (demonstration from the University of Hull—working with liquid nitrogen)
- Replacing and joining gas pipes (a demonstration from British Gas—who used the technique to make five-a-side goals for each school!)
- Making energy from gas (a demonstration of energy into electricity)
- Working with sound (Year 6 demonstrating a sound cannon)
- How helicopters work (investigating spinners by Years 3 and 4)
- Putting fires out safely (a demonstration by the fire service)
- What's in the air? (some experiments by Year 10 and 11 pupils)
- Flying a hot air balloon—(a demonstration by older pupils)
- Using pneumatics (hands-on exhibition of uses of air by Years 7 and 8)

As can be seen, pupils and adults were able to work alongside each other. The fair was run for five sessions over two days, including an evening session for parents. Each primary was given a session time where they could visit and this always coincided with some section of the secondary school, to ensure that not only were the displays from all phases, but so were the visitors.

The 16-page newspaper (although now looking rather dated) records pupils' enjoyment and enthusiasm, both for the topic and for working together.

The fair was a great success, and I thank Julie Broadbent (now Assistant Head at Endeavour, Hull) for the work she did in making it happen, and for reminding me of all the details.

I include the above example not as a model of perfect practice, but just as something that worked for us. I hope as you read this you were bringing to mind successful activities of which you are aware. This is a key point. There are good examples all over the country, sadly just not enough of them! I was keen to ensure that some examples from outside my own experience were included in this section, so I picked up the phone to speak to a group of people who spend their life looking for innovation. I spoke to my good friend Deryn Harvey, director of the Innovation Unit, who enthusiastically spoke of the unit's interest in improving transition. She put me in contact with Anne Diack, also from the unit, who below describes some research they carried out into improving transition through ICT.

Innovation, Innovation, Innovation

In 2004, The DfES Innovation Unit launched a 'disciplined innovation' project on transition. The aim was to investigate a fairly narrowly defined learning challenge—in this case the transition between Key Stage 2 and 3 in the subject discipline of ICT. Over 50 projects were submitted. From these, 13 were chosen, using a robust selection process, for their potential to help students maintain their level of expertise during the move from primary to secondary education.

We know both from research and from documenting the extensive filming that has been done in schools that younger pupils are often more expert in ICT than some of the older pupils, and also that the skills of some younger people can provide a challenge for teachers. We wanted to see if this innovation project could impact on pupil performance, as we know from a major research project that pupil performance often drops after transition from KS2 to KS3.

There was great variety in the selected projects. In Leeds, Year 6 students produced a story for an internet based radio station, with the help of Year 7 e buddies. The project involved 120 pupils and used specially designed characters in a radio drama about the experience of moving to the high school.

In Essex, an information exchange was arranged between staff and students in cluster schools, which also included the use of e buddies. Some 450 pupils were involved and the project enabled KS2 staff and students to become familiar with the geography and personnel of their receiving secondary school, as well as showing off the ICT work that Year 6 students were doing and enabling the staff to collaborate on ICT issues.

In Oxford, 200 pupils were involved in creating a ICT rich resource bank in Year 6 which was used for presentations on the environment in Year 7, and were also uploaded onto the local community online network. In Halifax, webcams were used to create links between the Year 6 and Year 7 pupils so that the younger children knew a familiar face when they arrived at the new school. The Year 6 children also had sessions in the ICT suite at the high school. This whole project involved 80 pupils.

In Durham, 170 pupils were involved in a common ICT curriculum for Years 6 and 7 together with a number of other initiatives that involved parents, promoting personalised learning and used classroom assistants and KS2/3 link assistants.

In North Yorkshire, almost 300 pupils were involved in creating a cross phase, multilingual TV programme to be shown in local schools. In Leeds, 40 pupils also made a programme about transition in which Year 7 pupils talked about their experiences of transition, and video was again used in the West Midlands where 60 pupils were involved in the project to address transition worries by getting the children to voice their worries and then showing how they found out the answers. The younger pupils also passed on their video editing skills to the older students.

In Bristol, dance linked to ICT was used by 40 pupils to express their emotions about moving to a new school.

In Northants, over 200 pupils worked on a project which linked past pupils with their old schools and encouraged them to broker the contact with Year 6 pupils through special projects linked to each feeder school, including creating a special online area which addressed the concerns of the younger pupils.

In Kent, 200 KS2 and KS3 pupils were involved in a collaborative science investigation which used ICT extensively.

In Staffordshire, a mobile ICT/multi media studio was used to develop ICT and media skills with 500 pupils, and to enable the new ICT teachers to have an idea of the levels of expertise of the Year 6 students, and in Wigan almost 600 pupils took part in a collaboratively designed ICT curriculum.

Teachers working on the projects took part in the Innovation Unit's Online Community, both during the submission process and also when the projects were running.

So did the projects work? In the project evaluation which took place in May 2005, all projects except one returned their evaluation forms giving 54 responses in total, and the overwhelming response was that the projects had worked well.

Teachers were asked to state what 'learning value' they thought their students got from the project on a scale of 1–10 where 10 is the highest response (i.e. the greatest learning) and 1 is the lowest?

 8 returns =10
10 returns = 9
21 returns = 8
14 returns = 5–7
 1 return = 4

The professional creativity demonstrated by the teachers who took part in these transition projects shows the wealth of talent and ingenuity that is available to the education system when the professional creativity of teachers is engaged. The Innovation Unit is now using this in its Next Practice programme which is covering the areas of leadership, personalisation, the whole school community and parents. You can find out more both about the transition projects mentioned above and The Innovation Unit's Next Practice programme at www.innovation unit.co.uk

This work by the Innovation Unit should be taken particularly seriously when you consider that the unit at this time was still part of the DfES. The issue of improving transition is clearly an important one, even in the highest circles! The focus on ICT, I believe, is perhaps a distraction, as my experience tells me that the topic is much less important than the approach.

These shorter projects are a very good place to start the journey of transition, but we must be clear that it is only a start. For sustained improvement longer relationships between the phases need to be built. The next section starts to investigate ways to do this.

How do we build strong foundations for transition?

This section contains a number of examples of longer term approaches that have proved to work for schools that have set themselves on a path to improve the relationships between the primary and secondary systems. Many of these examples have been refined over the years and are developing into routines which are slowly lessening the impact of transition for pupils.

Using specialist school status as a medium for transition

The majority of secondary schools are now specialist schools. This should be seen as an excellent route into transition. Primary colleagues reading this should remember that a large sum of money has been given to secondary schools particularly ear-marked for work with the community, of which you must be a major part. Therefore any work in this area should be funded from that money and **is not** a handout—in actual fact, you are doing the secondary a favour by spending it for them!

The Specialist Schools and Academies Trust (SSAT) are currently developing a programme of specialisms for primary schools—although I prefer to think of the growth of the current structure where specialism can be looked at throughout the whole of a child's schooling. The specialism from 3–18 has the added benefit that it can be looked at as enrichment, rather than cutting into the core workings of the primary school. This is particularly the case for specialisms such as business and enterprise, engineering, rural and vocational, where the subject can be broken down into a skills ladder by the family of schools to enhance provision across the whole area.

An excellent example of using specialism to support transition is Ridgewood School in Doncaster, where Headteacher Chris Hoyle believes that the work in engineering has been a major factor in developing positive and sustainable links in the family of schools.

Examples of the work include:

- Development of an Engineering Passport (this not only outlines key skills, it acts as a record of achievement in the specialism across all schools)
- Basic Skills support to all schools (specialist support is bought in to support national curriculum related topics, e.g. KS1—Designing and making a vehicle, KS2—Designing and making a vehicle powered by an electric motor)
- Community-based heritage projects (based around the locations of each primary school, e.g. for those near railways, a project was developed looking into how railways were used in World War 2; for others, model signals and points were constructed)
- STEM (engineering) award (a team of Engineering Ambassadors were created to produce DVDs, PowerPoint slides and animations to support any work in engineering)
- Model aeroplane flight challenge (mixed age groups of pupils form teams to design, construct and fly model aircraft)
- Engineer/technologist in residence (engineers placed in primary schools to offer hands-on experience for all pupils)
- Summer School (a two-week programme of events supporting engineering)

- Family Robot Day (an active day involving parents, grandparents and children in the design, making and testing of robots)

Full details of the projects and an example DVD is available from admin@ridgewood. doncaster.sch.uk

Another example of the strength of using specialist school specialisms at primary phase is shown at our own Serlby Park, where enterprise has become a major thread of transition. Susie Kent, a key cross-phase teacher picks up the story:

> Since we have been awarded Business and Enterprise status the junior site has set up both a healthy eating tuck shop and a radio station run and managed by Year 6 pupils. These have helped the pupils to develop the following Business and Enterprise traits: ingenuity, responsibility, creativity, team work and independence. This has also increased their confidence and ability to apply the numeracy strategy in real life situations. It has enabled them to develop their speaking and listening skills as they have to interact with pupils and staff alike.
>
> Now that the tuck shop is near to the end of its second successful year, numerous staff have noticed a change in the confidence of many of the employees. This has been especially noticed in children of low self esteem and in lower ability groups. They have shown qualities within the tuck shop that are hidden within the classroom, for example, shy, low ability children are working within the team to develop effective sales pitches and strategies for advertising produce.
>
> Being a 3–18 school allows the pupils to continue working in these projects whether it be through interviewing and training new employees or expanding the projects through other phases.

Perhaps the final word on the effectiveness of this kind of approach should be left to a Year 6 pupil, Celine Gair:

> When I started in Year 6, I applied for a job in the tuck shop. Two small serving windows had just been built using money from the Business and Enterprise department. I was one of the 16 cho sen out of the 50 who filled in an application form. If any of the students dropped out it was our job to look through the other forms and decide who could take their place.
>
> Our responsibilities included stock checks to see if we needed to order new stock, learning the prices, keeping everything tidy, counting money and looking after the keys.
>
> By working in the tuck shop it gave a chance to experience being in charge of running a busi ness. It taught us a lot about team work and how being able to work together is a very important part of life. It also gave us a chance to interact with the younger years. It let the teachers see that we were capable of working in a group and that we can be responsible whilst learning some skills. It gave us an insight into what our future careers might hold for us.
>
> I enjoyed working in the tuck shop. It was my best year in the junior site, an experience that I will never forget.

Although specialism is an excellent route into transition it is by no means the only way. It is therefore important to look at other examples of successful transition—next stop Eastwood Comprehensive.

Developing a personalised transition experience

A more traditional to approach the issues around creating effective transition is demonstrated by Eastwood Comprehensive School in Nottinghamshire. The Headteacher Chris Hasty has devolved responsibility to Joanne McCluskey (Senior Teaching Assistant responsible for transfer). A very systematic approach has been developed for a team of teaching assistants (TAs), who are given the time to make effective partnerships with their allocated primary school.

Points to note include:

- Transition starts for most in the September before their entry into secondary school
- A senior TA is invited to an annual review for all pupils in Year 5—enabling a transition individual education plan (IEP) to be developed well in advance
- All pupils from feeder schools are invited to attend summer school at the secondary
- Every pupil has their own personalised transition plan. This states what will happen for the year before transition, when and by whom. It contains the names of teachers familiar to the pupil as well as new ones involved in transition. This means every pupil and parent has a full understanding of the transition process from the outset
- A roadshow visits each school in the autumn term, showing items of uniform, musical instruments and answering practical questions about the 'new' school
- Early taster sessions are held in the secondary school for every feeder school and a range of further visits throughout Year 6
- Personalised activity books are produced for every child relating the new school to their own experience. Colour photos of key new staff are included, and the pupils are encouraged to use the book with their parents over the months before the move

A CD-ROM game is also being developed with Clicker 5 technology. The game attempts to answer questions and concerns that Year 6 pupils are faced with on transition. A team of Year 7 pupils have played a key role in developing this. The CD also provides pupils with a map and many different photographs of the school building. (More information is available from the school on 01773 786212.) This approach is producing some very positive responses from pupils and staff, but it should be noted that this is an example of traditional style transition done very well. This same approach, if not delivered with empathy and consistency, can simply reinforce the big school/little school mentality.

The key to the success of the Eastwood approach is the frequency, reliability and personalisation of the contact. The more facts a child has the less likely they are to have their fears fed by rumour. I still remember the worry on a Year 6's face as he asked me about the ritual of being pushed down the hill by older pupils—it took me a while to realise that he was referring to a slight lump in an area of grass that had somehow taken on mountainous dimensions in his mind. Every child approaching the change of school will have their own hill—effective transition must be about flattening these hills. Making molehills out of mountains?

Transition is not just for the summer term—it's for life!

Hazel Beales from Market Weighton School describes their journey to effective transition, which combines a mixture of the approaches described in the previous case studies:

At last you have made successful contact with your partner schools. You have consulted, collaborated and cooperated, and your transition or bridging project is in place. You are happy with the lessons at either end of the process, your social visits and your taster days are all booked, what else is there possibly left to do? Well, there's so much more to learn and discover. I would strongly suggest that transition does not end after the handover of the precious cargo, our students.

If transition is to be a successful and continuous process, then discussion and dialogue should continue beyond the September transfer. Maintain your contact with the partner schools and try to ensure that there are meetings at least once in the autumn and spring terms, one for review and the other for planning or perhaps developing new projects. Contact is essential and should be maintained once the barriers are broken down.

Here in Market Weighton we have visited all our partner schools to study how they are using guided reading as means to improve reading skills and comprehension. This was very enlightening and we have tried to adapt some of the techniques into our own teaching. However, secondary schools are far more bound by the timetable and finding a weekly, let alone daily spot to work on reading skills has proved nigh on impossible. Most primary schools use the first 15 minutes of the afternoon session, which has the added bonus of calming the students after lunch and getting them back into a mindset for work. Perhaps the suggested changes to secondary school timetables might prove helpful.

If you have formed good relationships with your partner schools, then team teaching is another really beneficial and enjoyable process. We have found it easier to do this in the primary schools as they have far more difficulties regarding cover. Team teaching is enjoyable and collaborative planning means that secondary and primary colleagues have a shared expectation regarding outcomes. We secondary teachers frequently underestimate the capabilities of our Year 7 students and the same may be the case for teachers of Year 3. These sessions also allow us to see each other's strengths and also are occasions for dialogue regarding how to manage the behaviour and learning of individual students who will be joining us the following September.

Some schools, perhaps yours, have a designated teacher in charge of transition who visits their partner schools regularly throughout the year. This is the ideal situation, but is expensive in terms of time and money. I believe that the more teachers who are willing to give up time to visit their partner schools, be it primary or secondary, the better, as the sharing of expertise is that much greater. The latter is often the case with PE where primary schools do not necessarily have the necessary facilities or expertise to extend their students' learning or experience. Here, older students can also become involved and we have found the Junior Sports' Leader programme a very effective tool at KS4 and have now extended the work to the Sixth Form, who are currently studying for their Community Sports' Leader Award. It is hoped that these awards will be extended to literacy, numeracy and the sciences in the near future and will further improve the transitional experience of primary students.

Although we also have a great deal to learn from our primary colleagues, they are under pressure to teach a wide range of subjects which might not necessarily be their particular strength or

Longcroft School & Performing Arts College
4–19 Assessment Levels
Dance, Drama and Music

	1	2	3	4	5
Making	You are unsure of your ideas and often hesitant and wary of others.	You offer many ideas, are thoughtful and can follow others	You share ideas and support others and your work is becoming more detailed.	You are becoming more inventive and your ideas are more original. You watch and learn from others, evaluating your work as you go along.	You are a leader, creative, experimental and compromise with others.
	Advice: Don't be frightened of making mistakes. Be confident.	**Advice:** Make a difference and give even more ideas. You don't always have to follow others.	**Advice:** Try to discuss your ideas in more depth and experiment more.	**Advice:** Keep focused and try to become completely fluent.	**Advice:** Continue to develop your team skills and the quality of your creative ideas.
Performing	You are making your first steps.	You are developing your performance skills and are aware of an audience.	You feel secure and give a more confident performance.	You are expressive in your performance and more awae of your audience.	You are fluent and very confident. An audience enjoys your performance.
	Advice: Don't be afraid to take even bigger steps.	**Advice:** Remember that practice makes perfect.	**Advice:** You've got it. Now listen to your feedback and try to make the changes.	**Advice:** You are doing well. What performance techniques could you improve to move to the higher level?	**Advice:** What else do you think an audience would like to see or hear?
Evaluating	You can *describe* the lesson.	You can explain some of your ideas and progress.	You can accurately explain how you improved your work.	You make informative detailed and reflective comments.	You use specialist language when evaluating and often relate your work to others.
	Advice: Explain your ideas more.	**Advice:** Explain all of the problems and how you solved them.	**Advice:** Start comparing your work to other pupils'.	**Advice:** Try to use specialist terms in your evaluation.	**Advice:** Can you use ideas from other people to solve any problems you may have had?

talent—subjects such as art, music, dance and drama. Here collaborative work can be a great help and local specialist secondary schools can provide the answer. Transition in these areas may prove a headache if you are not really sure about levels of assessment. Even in secondary schools this can be a problem if, for example, you are an English specialist who is required to teach and assess drama without previous training. Never fear, there are schools working collaboratively to produce user friendly assessment documents for students and teachers at all the key stages. Longcroft School and Performing Arts College in Beverley, East Riding of Yorkshire, for example, is in the final stages of producing an assessment level document for students from the ages of 4–19, which was piloted as of September 2007. If you are interested in receiving such a useful transition document please contact sara.mcintyre@longcroft.eriding.net and she will be happy to help you. The document has been several years in the making and has involved close cooperation with Longcroft's partner primary, junior and infant schools, and we are eventually hoping to extend aspects of the assessment into the Market Weighton area.

Another excellent tool for aiding effective transition is to allow staff to visit schools and observe lessons at the different key stages. It is a means to observe and assess the different layers of learning that take place. Once you have a good relationship with your partner schools they are far less threatened by such visits. Alternatively, why not become a governor and you will be positively welcomed into all aspects of the school's life. I recently visited a Year 2 classroom with a Graduate Teacher Programme secondary English student and by strange coincidence the children were studying anthropomorphic stories (stories where animals adopt human characteristics), a topic we were working on with Year 7 students at the time. It was fascinating to observe how the teacher tackled this subject and how skilful questioning elicited really excellent responses from these 6 and 7 year olds. As we were studying the same topic with our students, it became clear that we are building up layers of understanding and encouraging children to build up a range of skills which they can apply at all stages of education.

If visits to schools are difficult in your case, then continue to invite staff from your partner schools to regular transition meetings as I suggested earlier. These meetings should have a definite purpose; many will be about the logistics of the transition that year but equally they can be a forum to discuss topical subjects or problems. We have recently been discussing the fall in performance over the summer holiday between the key stages, for example.

Finally, if your partner schools use assessment books for written assignments, then why not consider transferring these to their next school. Students and teachers will therefore have a record of previous progress at the different key stages, so any 'slippage' or areas of weakness are more evident and can be addressed earlier. Primary schools often rightly complain that too little notice is taken of the records and details they send to the secondary school—too often the boxes being consigned to dusty store cupboards and we secondary school teachers not even being aware of their existence. To continue an assessment book or record scheme seems an eminently sensible way forward and we gradually intend to have an agreed scheme of assessment in English. It is also ecologically more sound; another area where infant, junior and primary schools lead the way for many secondary schools to follow.

Transition is never ending and should not be consigned to simply the summer term. Once links are in place, the opportunities are enormous and we must constantly seek to explore every avenue where collaboration and cooperation will lead to us becoming better teachers than we already are, but, much more importantly, will ultimately lead to improving the transitional experience for all of our students.

Hazel is an enthusiastic teacher who is passionate about pupils—this being the key to her success. She can be contacted at Market Weighton School on 01430 873450.

I believe that personal experience of the different phases of education should be a compulsory part of each teacher's yearly staff development. For many, the only experience they have of the different age groups is in a week-long placement during their teacher training year—occurring before they have had much experience of their chosen age specialism, therefore losing potential for comparison and long-term benefit.

I hope some of you reading this will now be interested to dig a little deeper and try to understand in more detail the massive potential benefits for both primary and secondary schools from the longer projects. For this reason, I now include a number of case studies. In these studies the key person responsible for the activity describes their own story, why they did it and the lessons they believe arise from the activity. Read the studies in the way one gazes at a sumptuous buffet, looking to find the bits that appeal to you, not trying to scoff the lot!

Case study 1

At Serlby Park, we have encouraged teachers to go one step further and partner with teachers in other phases. Below is an account of such a partnership from Joy Sweeney (Assistant Principal—infant phase) and Ian Peach (TLR1—Teaching and Learning (secondary)). Joy outlines the process.

Using thinking skills as a cross-phase tool
by Joy Sweeney and Ian Peach

Staff volunteers from all three phases were sought and a teaching and learning group was established. I was very keen to be part of this group as I am passionate about the concept of all through education and welcomed the opportunity to develop cross phase links. Meetings were scheduled throughout the year and an agenda was drafted. Foci included:

- How to interpret learning style analyses
- How to produce group profiles from learning styles analyses
- How to produce learning maps for left and right brain dominant students
- The use of tactile learning tools for kinaesthetic and tactile learners
- Assessment for learning
- Interactive whiteboards as a learning tool

Meeting with consultants

Early in September 2005 two KS3/4 strategy consultants met with our group to present a brief outline of the KS4 Learning Strategy Project. They worked with the group to develop an action plan to take the theories outlined by Barbara Prashnig in *The Power of Diversity* into classroom practice. (Every teacher and governor at Serlby Park were given a copy of this book during the amalgamation of the school.)

We were informed that funding was available to enable teachers to further develop the project during school hours and that we would have their support throughout the project.

It was decided that the staff would pair up with someone from another phase who had similar interests. The aim was to plan individual lessons together which would take account of the learning styles indicated by the Prashnig data and which would incorporate the elements of effective lessons. Each pair would decide on a focus class to trial this work with and might also target specific individuals within the class. I teach Foundation Stage 2 children and I chose to pair up with an English teacher from Key Stage 3 with a Year 9 class. It was agreed that we would meet with our consultant in order to plan a lesson for each of our classes.

Planning meetings

We discussed the data from the learning style analyses that the older pupils had completed. From this we concluded that effective lessons should plan to access a range of teaching and learning styles. We also noted that whilst we might choose to teach particularly challenging things in a preferred way, we would also be doing the pupils a disservice if we did not support them in developing other ways of learning as well.

Developing thinking skills strategies would certainly meet this range of styles and so we decided to adopt this as our focus for the series of lessons that we would plan and deliver. We would then have a direct comparison between Year 9 pupils and Foundation 2 pupils.

We needed to clarify the terminology for learning objectives and outcomes in order to have consistency in both phases. It was agreed that we would use KNOW, UNDERSTAND, CAN DO as useful prompts. Differentiation of outcomes would be met by using ALL, MOST, SOME. In order to develop respect for, and an understanding of, the issues related to the different phases, we decided to observe each other's teaching. The consultant would observe both of us and we would then feedback to each other afterwards.

Ian adds a secondary teacher's analysis of the process:

The coaching cycle

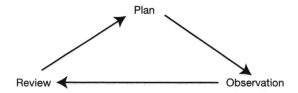

This coaching process created a non threatening and non judgmental approach and gave colleagues the chance to trial ideas and have them observed and reviewed in order to develop practice.

The planning sessions were extremely important as they provided time for teacher discussion and the sharing of ideas. In a number of evaluation meetings this area was seen by teachers to be extremely beneficial, as the following quote demonstrates.

When asked the question: 'What were the main benefits of the strategy?' one group replied: 'Working together, understanding the different approaches across phases.'

During the observation the observers were encouraged to team teach and to become involved in the lesson rather than become mere passive observers. Pupils were questioned by the consult ant during the course of the lesson to discover what they enjoyed and which areas helped them to learn.

The lesson was then reviewed straightaway by the consultant and the two teachers. Areas of strength were looked at, as were weaknesses and strategies which had not worked. The next planning session was then agreed along with any proposals for the lesson.

We made sure that all involved were familiar with the VAKT (**V**isual, **A**uditory, **K**inaesthetic and **T**actile) system of analyzing teaching and learning styles (for further details see www. droppingthebaton.com). Most members of the group felt fairly comfortable with the visual and auditory aspect of the learning styles model used, however they were less secure on the tactile and kinaesthetic aspects. The group was therefore actively encouraged to develop the use of tactile learning tools such as:

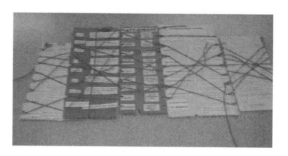

- Learning circles
- Wraparounds
- Flip chutes
- Electro boards
- Card tasks
- Board games

Added to these were a range of thinking skills activities based on the work of David Leat (avail able from Kingston Publishing) and other kinaesthetic methods, such as concept circles and opinion lines. The use of thinking maps was also piloted by this group. Many students learn best when utilising tactile and kinaesthetic resources and many of the methods used were transfer able right across the age range.

During the cycle, regular teaching and learning meetings were held. The purpose of these was twofold: firstly to check on the progress of the strategy and to identify any problem areas, and secondly to share teaching methodologies with other members of the group.

These meetings were vital in ensuring that pairs actually met as communication across the three sites could be an issue. To ensure that these meetings took place they were scheduled in the meetings calendar and reminders were sent out in the internal post along with minutes of previ ous meetings and agendas for the next. Evaluations from the project proved very positive.

Personal thoughts from Joy

At the time that we were planning these lessons I was conscious that the number of children in my class would change. We admit children into Foundation Stage 2 three times throughout the year. My class would therefore increase from 14 children to 21 children in January. At the planned time of my lesson observation there would be seven children who would only have been in my class for a fortnight. I felt it important that the observers needed to be aware of this as it impacts on the personal, social and emotional development of all the children in the class.

Learning in the Foundation Stage is based around six areas:

- Personal, social and emotional development
- Communication, language and literacy
- Mathematical development
- Knowledge and understanding of the world
- Physical development
- Creative development

I needed to explain that we focused on a topic each half term and that all the skills from the different areas of learning were planned around this. Often there would be combination of different areas of learning where the children would be applying their skills, knowledge and developing further understanding. This is a very different approach to learning in Year 9.

My plan for the first lessons is shown opposite.

Feedback from my living map activity

Each group was supported by an adult. The children enjoyed the activity and coped very well with the statements. Natural discussions arose when there was a difference of opinion. All the children were willing to give reasons for their choices, including one child who put his hand up and couldn't answer but said he was still thinking.

We felt that the children could have coped with even more ambiguous statements. This is an area I plan to develop further.

We also discussed whether the children could have done this activity without an adult helper. We thought that it would be possible if we ensured that there was a good reader in each group. Rules for working as a team would need to be reinforced so that one person would not prevail in the group.

Feedback from Year 9 living map activity

The pupils enjoyed this activity as it also appealed to the more tactile learners.

Group work with the statements led to stimulating discussions and they were able to justify their reasons. It was obvious that they were applying prior learning very effectively and they had a sound knowledge of the play and the characters.

Spring term 1 topic: My Home and Village **Theme:** My Home **Story focus:** Goldilocks and the Three Bears	
Learning outcomes	All will have made a circle thinking map with pictures Most will use pictures and attempt to write five words Some will use more than five words from a word bank
Learning objectives	Know what a circle thinking map is Understand how to use it to draw things in your bedroom Can make a circle thinking map for your bedroom
Skills to be developed	Observation Speaking and listening Defining in context thinking skills Reasoning thinking skills Social skills Decision making skills
Introduction	Remind the children of prior learning. Explain they will be making models of their bedroom later in the day
Main part Visual learners	**Thinking strategy-living maps** Divide children into groups of four or five Give each group a picture of The Three Bears' Bedroom and a selection of ambiguous statements on individual cards, e.g. • Daddy Bear likes to keep clean • It belongs to Mummy Bear • Baby Bear loves this • We are nice and warm • You can open this Ask the children to stick each card onto the picture somewhere Help the children to read the cards if necessary, encourage them to discuss and explain Discuss each group's decisions, encourage them to agree or disagree with each other's choices, always giving reasons
	Brain Break Activity
Auditory learners	**Thinking skill—defining in context** Recap on some items in The Three Bears' bedroom. Explain that we are going to make models of our bedrooms later and that we need to remember what is in our own bedrooms Ask the children to sit opposite a partner Explain that they need to talk about five things that are in their bedroom and then swap over Explain that they are going to record what is in their bedrooms by making a circle thinking map and that they will be using this map that afternoon to help them make their bedrooms Children to make their circle maps
Kinaesthetic learners	Children to use plasticine, Lego, constructional material to make beds, etc.
Plenary	Share some of the circle maps with the children Remind children of the task this afternoon Sing the Goldilocks Rap!

Lesson outline for Year 9

Much Ado About Nothing Act 3, Scene 2; Act 4, Scene 1, lines 1–163	
Learning objectives	To know what inference is To understand how to be able to infer in Act 3, Scene 2, of *Much Ado About Nothing*
Learning outcomes	All will be able to write an explanation of a section of Act 3, Scene 2 Most will write an explanation of the scene and justify it Some will apply technique to the whole scene
Starter Visual	Display a picture on the whiteboard and ask three questions. What do we know? What can we infer? What do we want to know?
Main part	Use the key scene and ask pupils to match ambiguous statements to different characters Work in groups and feed back to the class Justify the reasons Write an explanation of some of the statements and justify them
Plenary	Show a picture, either the same or a different one, and ask the class what are we inferring from this?

My observations

It was interesting for me to witness this level of discussion and compare it to the 4 and 5 year olds that I teach. The same thinking strategy was being used to equal effect.

I was very conscious that these pupils would not be following this thread of learning for several days; this was in stark contrast to my class who would be continuing it the same afternoon.

I was beginning my journey of developing respect for some of the issues that my secondary colleagues face on a daily basis:

- Swiping in at the start of a lesson
- Not having a pencil or pen
- Constraints of time
- Chatting with peers about 'teenage' issues
- Clock watching towards the end of a lesson
- Bells
- Two minute respite before teaching the next year group with a totally different focus
- The inability to connect/apply the learning in a different area

Summing up

Several more lessons were jointly planned, delivered and observed. Areas for development were welcomed and incorporated in future lessons. It was agreed that we would share our good practice with colleagues in both phases and discuss within the teaching and learning groups how this work could be sustained the following year.

We were then invited to give a 30 minute presentation of our joint experiences to a Key Stage 4 learning strategy celebration event which would be held later on in the year. This proved to be another new experience. It enabled me to share the philosophy of primary education with other secondary teachers and heads from across the county.

Conclusion

Being part of an all through learning environment is fascinating. As a teacher of young children we naturally make cross curricular links with all areas of learning. Children have many opportunities to apply and transfer skills. This leads to a deeper understanding. The secondary approach is very different, although changes are afoot!

I have developed a greater knowledge of a different phase of education and formed new friendships. As more colleagues embrace pairing up and sharing lessons, I feel confident that we will all develop mutual respect and be able to learn from one another. There are many cross phase projects being planned with both pupils and staff working in collaboration. I believe that more emphasis should be based on the acquisition of skills and competencies leading to more personalised learning. In our rapidly changing world we need to foster a love of learning that will enable young people to embrace their futures.

Case study 2

At Serlby Park we have developed a leadership structure which includes a number of cross-phase posts. One of these is held by Louise Edwards, who leads dance and drama across the whole 3–18 age group. She has a unique opportunity to understand the issues of transition, and her account describes the insight she has gained.

Potato printing through the ages
by Louise Edwards

How can differing approaches in primary and secondary be drawn closer together to allow a more seamless transition? At Serlby Park one idea we are trailing in order to combat this has been to introduce an alternative curriculum for Year 7 students. This has worked by a team of teachers from both primary and secondary creating and delivering an integrated curriculum for the first two hours of every day. On the whole it is proving to be a successful programme. It is too early in the programme to decide whether it will have an impact on the children's learning long term but as a vehicle for seamless transition from the primary to the secondary it seems to be working effectively. There is still the issue at present that after year 7 the students will return to a full subject based curriculum.

In the next page is an example of some planning used by Year 7 teachers. It is taken from the International Primary Curriculum model. It shows a selection of themed lessons based on how the brain works. The activities offer opportunities for visual, auditory and kinaesthetic learning.

Learning how to learn workshop

Outline plans

Lesson 1
- Knowledge harvest—find out previous learning from pupils
- Big picture—introduce topic and learning outcomes, including pupil self assessment
- Start class display, learning map on wall to evidence learning as a group

Lesson 2
- Independent research about the brain (library/internet)
- Presentation of facts in VAK styles
- Make a brain like substance/model of brain

Lesson 3
- Identify four lobes of brain and the purpose of each
- Use brace map to record information
- Stroop effect/optical illusions

Lesson 4
- Neurons
- Make models using beads/string and group models using rope

As a secondary dance/drama teacher I appreciate the constraints under which the secondary system works. Classroom space, resources, timetabling and the pressure to get students through GCSEs and A level exams (to mention a few) all play a part in how the system has developed. It is also important to say that secondary teachers teach their specialism in isolation because they are imparting knowledge and skills at a higher level. It would be difficult to take on teaching other subjects outside of their specialism because of this. However, maybe there are ways in which subject leaders could communicate better to ensure skills and knowledge progression.

One way I feel this could be improved is by teachers developing a clearer understanding of skills and knowledge that are being taught in other departments. This knowledge would then allow them to identify links to their subject so they can expand on prior learning and plan more effectively. It will also encourage the children to make links in their learning, which will help them to apply its relevance to everyday life. Working in this way could lead to schemes of work being developed across departments. This could diminish the amount of knowledge individual subject teachers have to teach and leave more time for working on skills.

My experience as a teacher in both primary and secondary has developed my understanding that on the whole children don't learn effectively when they are taught in a segmented manner. They learn in isolation and struggle to apply their skills and knowledge outside of the situation in which they have been taught.

As a primary practitioner in the early years, thematic teaching was an everyday occurrence. This was because of the need to keep reiterating learning objectives in many different ways so the children remembered what they had learnt and could apply it to their experiences outside of school. It was also to keep them engaged and help concentration. For example, a topic on transport could include doing a traffic survey and presenting the results on a graph, creating a train station role play area which involved writing tickets, paying with money, taking on driver and passenger roles, etc., exploring how things move, exploring how bodies travel across space. With the introduction of Excellence and Enjoyment and the new primary frameworks for teaching literacy and mathematics that have just been introduced, education in the whole of the primary phase is moving closer and closer to an integrated approach to learning. It therefore seems strange why, if so much effort is placed on delivering this type of curriculum in the primary phase, the secondary model of teaching is traditionally very different.

Teaching approaches

Another area where primary and secondary practices differ is in their approach to teaching and learning. This again is in part to do with the differing structures but I also feel it is often because there is a belief that pupils get 'too old' for a lot of practices they have been exposed to at primary school.

From teaching across the ages I am of the opinion that many secondary age students often need to continue to experience the types of approaches below the keep them engaged and to ensure their preferred learning style is being catered for.

Rhymes, songs and raps

How many nursery rhymes or children songs do you know? Chances are most of us know quite a few and the likelihood is we learnt them at primary school. This suggests to me that the power of music on learning and retaining that learning is immense. Putting a melody or rhythm to an area of learning cements the ideas in the brain more than just reading the information or hearing it. Obviously the style of song will change depending on the age of the children but this offers the teacher an opportunity to tap into music styles and groups that are popular with the students. Why not change the words to a well known chart hit? Better still get the students to make up their own song or rap to remember some key words!

Rap examples

Here is a rap I devised with my Year 1 children to get them to come and sit on the carpet more quickly and get ready to learn. It can have actions to follow the words that the class can help to make up.

Come and sit on the carpet if you want to be cool
If you wander around you'll look like a fool!
Eyes on the teacher, bodies to front,
Please don't wriggle and listen to this riddle!
Are you ready to learn? One
Are you ready to learn? Two
Are you ready to learn? Three
Brains in gear—WE'RE READY!!!

Here's one I created for my GCSE Dance group to help them remember the compositional process. As above, I find that it helps students to remember the words if they make up actions.

Choose your stimulus and improvise
Selecting the best ideas is really wise
Form movement motifs to fit your idea
Develop them but make it clear
Now you look at forming sections
Think about the pace and length in your selection
Structuring the whole dance is the next job you must do
Binary, rondo, narrative to name a few
Check your structure is right for your theme
Find an ending that works like a dream
Then your job is almost done
Rehearsal your piece till it's A1!

Actions/movement/dance

Similarly to rhymes, songs and raps, getting pupils' bodies moving is also an important way to ensure they are learning through all their senses. In the primary sector children are given more opportunities to express themselves with their bodies because they have classrooms that are not full of desks and can be modified for learning tasks at different points in the day. In second ary schools classrooms are often used by more than one subject group and therefore have to accommodate different numbers of pupils, which means they are mainly filled with desks. I think the classroom environment is therefore limiting the possibilities for movement in the secondary sector. However, I do feel that classroom spaces could be made more flexible by creating a number of classrooms in subject blocks that are empty to accommodate lessons that include movement.

Here is picture of a Year 6 classroom that has been designed by the children. It has desks for working at but also a tent with cushions and lots of empty floor space. This layout is altered regularly in consultation with the pupils depending upon the topic they are doing and how they wish to work.

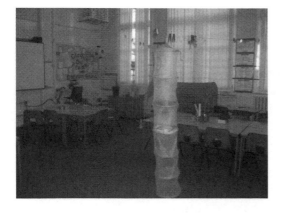 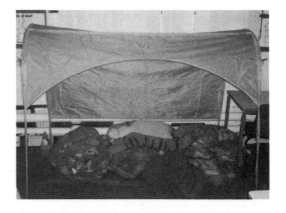

Another reason why dance and movement aren't used enough in the secondary sector, in my opinion, is teachers' lack of knowledge, skills and confidence in this area. In primary, teachers are used to teaching all subjects from maths to PE. They are often less inhibited about using their bodies as a method of expressing an idea. I must mention, however, that despite this my experience in primary still demonstrates to me that many primary practitioners lack confidence in teaching dance/movement as a pure subject. This suggests that there is still a lot of room for developing good and regular practice in this area in primary. I feel therefore in both sectors there needs to be a lot more time and money spent on developing teachers' abilities to be confident in using their bodies as medium for expression.

Here is picture of some infant children dancing. They are responding with their bodies to a piece of lively music. They are engrossed in the task and are keen to try out moving their bodies in different ways.

The messy stuff!

My title 'Potato printing through the ages' was inspired by this section. One of the main reasons I trained to be a primary teacher in the early years is that I loved to do arts and crafts activities. I looked forward to the times when the paints, glue, collage materials and Play Doh came out. As I mentioned before, the more flexible timetable allowed this to happen frequently in my Year 1 classroom. This wasn't just in 'art' sessions but was integrated into all curriculum subjects where appropriate.

I found that by approaching learning objectives in a creative manner the children were more engaged and enthused about what they were learning. I feel that tactile activities are often side lined in secondary due to individual classroom resources and the restrictions of the timetable. I feel that more teachers in secondary would integrate these types of activities into their lessons if each department had resources to accommodate this. I don't believe it is enough to offer the children these kinds of experiences just in art as we are missing the potential of tactile teaching methods to deepen understanding and engage young people.

I also feel teachers in the secondary sector are sometimes wary of doing these types of activities because they are unsure of effective strategies for classroom management. This is again where further training needs to be offered.

Classroom and school environment

Through working in many primary and secondary schools one big difference that stands out to me is the physical and social environment in which children learn. In terms of physical environ ment primary schools are on the whole more colourful, bright and welcoming. Each classroom has its own identity and individuality and school achievements are celebrated through corridor displays, etc. I believe this again relates to children having their own classroom as well as the fact that generally primary schools have fewer pupils on roll. I feel it is true to say that primary teach ers are often more aware of how the physical environment effects the children's learning and well being in school. This is maybe because they are dealing with younger children and have to address how child centred their environment is to ensure they settle and are able to learn.

Here are some examples of ways that primary teachers make the classroom environment child centred.

On the left you can see a 'Star of the Week' and 'Carer of the Week' board. Each week a different child's name is chosen to go under the two headings. Having this system in the class gives them a weekly goal to work towards which is celebrated by displaying their name for everyone to see. On the right there is a visual timetable. This has symbols to represent different lessons through the day. It helps children to see what is happening throughout the day. The visual symbols are useful for the children who struggle to read text. It helps them to be independent so they are not always relying on the teacher.

In terms of social environment I believe there are many differences between primary and second ary. Due to the age of pupils in primary the approach from staff is more child centred and caring. It is a home away from home where most children know all the staff and have opportunities to engage with pupils of all ages. As they have one classroom teacher they build strong relation ships with that person, who in turn gets to know them on a personal and academic level. In secondary, due to the numbers of pupils this approach can be lost. It takes longer for children to meet all the staff and although they have a form tutor they have lots of teachers in a week. This can lead to personal and academic problems being overlooked or missed. There is also less interaction between year groups. Unless the school has a big main hall the assemblies etc. are split into lower and upper school. I feel this has a big impact upon the well being of some pupils. One of the main reasons Serlby Park became a 3–18 school was to address this issue. Activities such as cross phase projects and cross phase teaching are helping to bridge the gap between staff and pupils from the primary and secondary sites. Trying to create a common approach to pastoral systems as well as using systems such as Sleuth (a computerised database) to track pupils' behaviour through school is also addressing the need to place more emphasis on the social environment of school.

Concluding statements

In conclusion I think that there are many differences between the primary and secondary approaches to education that hinder effective transition for pupils. Although some strategies are being used to try and combat this, such as transition schemes of work, open days where pupils can visit their secondary school and, in the case of 3–18 schools such as Serlby Park, cross phase teaching and projects, there still seems to be some segregation between the primary and secondary phases of education. As this section reveals, this is often because of how primary and secondary schools are traditionally run due to numbers of students and the constraints of exams. However, I hope that I have raised some points for reflection and discussion about what more could be done to ease transition and share good and effective practice across the phases. I believe that until some of these issues are addressed we will continue to see a drop in pupil achievement and enthusiasm to learn from primary to secondary, and this will in turn impact upon people's motivation to continue learning throughout their lives.

Case study 3

Not all transition is successful on its first attempt, and this further contribution by Hazel Beales, Head of English at Market Weighton School, is a great example of the benefits of persistence. The focus on questioning skills was a stroke of genius, enabling a common ground of development for all professionals involved.

'To be or not to be? That is the question'
by Hazel Beales

Before I begin I'd better introduce your guide to the world of transition and questioning. I do not claim to be an expert, but I am an experienced classroom teacher, having spent the last 27 years teaching in a small (750 student) comprehensive school in the East Riding of Yorkshire. Market Weighton is best known by aficionados of The Guinness Book of Records as the birthplace of the tallest man in England, one William Bradley (1787–1820), and the soil of one of our near neighbours, Holme upon Spalding Moor, had the dubious honour of producing the largest carrot in the United Kingdom, or so my students tell me.

I may not have gone far geographically in terms of my own career, but over the last 10 years I have travelled far in my understanding of the importance of cooperation and dialogue between secondary and primary colleagues and students if transition is to be effective. Along the way, my understanding of the role of effective questioning skills in improving teaching and learning has also been enhanced and I think I've become a better classroom practitioner as a direct result. I do not claim to be the new Messiah with regard to questioning—there is a great deal of information in government publications and on the internet about the subject—but I do have practical experience of establishing effective links between a cluster of schools and of the use of questioning to improve classroom practice at all key stages. I may be preaching to the already converted; I do know there is some excellent transition work and questioning going on in the wider world of education, but this case study may prove helpful to those who are struggling to establish links with their partner schools or those who are seeking to improve them.

This is our story.

Transition and how to fall at the first hurdle

Imagine the scenario … Your LEA has decided that transition needs to be a higher priority. You and your secondary colleagues are invited to a meeting to discuss writing a transition project and then piloting it with your partner schools. It all seems a brilliant idea. You are paired with a colleague from another secondary school and you are to recruit other interested parties in your schools to the transition cause.

You return to school, full of the enthusiasm of the convert, and you settle on your target—in my case the Head of History, Maxine Squire, who is to feature later in the journey to successful transition. At Wolfreton School, a 2,000 student comprehensive in the affluent leafy suburbs on the outskirts of Hull, Linda Downes, a fellow English teacher, is recruiting an enthusiastic young geographer, Richard Ness. Wolfreton School has a huge catchment area and in that year, 2001, they had an intake of students from approximately 19 schools, whereas we at Market Weighton only had four, Mount Pleasant C. of E. Junior School and St Mary's Roman Catholic Primary in the town itself, and Newbald Primary School and Holme Upon Spalding Moor Primary School in neighbouring villages. But with the naivety born of enthusiasm, we thought that the writing of the piece would be the hardest part of the process.

The resulting transition unit, A Roman Journey, was a cross curricular work of art and we had great fun putting it together. But have you spotted the fatal flaw in the plan yet? If you have, then what happened next should come as no surprise. When I approached the head teacher of Mount Pleasant Junior School, Ian Merryweather, a man of great experience and wisdom, regarding the implementation of the transition project, he quite rightly turned me down. Ian cited the fact that primary and junior schools were inundated with new initiatives and the staff would not welcome another imposition, for that was what it was.

We in the secondary sector often fall into the trap of patronising our primary colleagues, deluding ourselves that 'we know best', and there is still the misguided belief in some quarters that secondary schools are bigger and better in every way. This is absolutely not the case. We have a great deal to learn from the practices in our primary schools. Ian brought us down to earth and I thank him for it, for if he had agreed to implement the original transition project, we would not have embarked on our new voyage of discovery, which led to the infinitely superior and adaptable work on questioning skills in our cluster schools.

If you are wondering what happened to A Roman Journey, which does have its merits as a cross curricular themed bridging project for use either in transition or in Years 6 or 7, it can still be found, as I discovered recently, at www.eriding.net/history/romans.shtml.

A question without a satisfactory answer

I suppose I have always been committed to the principles of transition without at times even knowing it. For the past 10 or more years I have been a member of the governing bodies of Market Weighton Infant School and Mount Pleasant Junior School. I have found this an invaluable experience as it has allowed me an insight into what drives these key stages, and I have had the pleasure of working closely with my primary colleagues. It has also allowed me to see the progression that takes place between the key stages and the problems of transition brought about by a change of school building, teachers and ethos. The role of the governor is an invaluable one and I would urge more of my colleagues to become involved. For me it was my first step on the journey.

Few teachers have anything positive to say about the ogre that is Ofsted. The mention of the name strikes fear in us all. However, I do have reason to be very grateful to the team who visited the local infant school in the summer of 2002. The report was a very favourable and fair one. Moreover, it highlighted that the quality of questioning in the classroom was variable and that teachers were too reliant on closed questions and this did not allow for the children to expand their responses or give them opportunities to think more critically or thoughtfully. There were some examples of very good practice, but they could name no names. Questioning was to be a focus for improvement.

It became clear from speaking to other schools that had visits from the beast that this was a focus at the time. As the junior schools and secondary school were due a visit too, I began to worry. How guilty was I of asking questions that did not elicit the best responses from my stu dents? What types of questions did I ask of my students? Was my questioning too focused on content rather than understanding and application? What types of questions were my students asking me, and each other? What I could I do to improve the situation? The questions were end less. I invite you to ask yourself these questions too. Are you comfortable with the answers? Is there, to coin a phrase much loved by my former teachers, 'room for improvement'?

I went to the follow up meeting armed with one vital question. 'What training was the LEA pro viding to improve the quality of questioning in East Riding schools?' A thoughtful silence was followed by a 'none' answer. As far as the link adviser was aware, there was no such training available and the issue of questioning, albeit vital, was not at that time a priority. A challenge if ever there was one. If the LEA were not providing the necessary INSET, we would have to help ourselves.

At this point we had two lucky breaks: Sarah Kay Wood, the deputy headteacher of the infant school took up the mantle on their behalf (and you can read her vital contribution to the improve ment of questioning in the Market Weighton Cluster further on) and then my collaborator in the original failed transition project, Maxine Squire, was appointed to a consultant post in the LEA. Maxine began researching the importance of effective questioning in the classroom as part of her role and here she was aided and abetted by the new and enthusiastic KS3 literacy consult ant, Jane Lodge, and Jane Dixon, literacy consultant for KS1 and KS2. All the components for change were assembled; we now just needed to get all the schools on board. A fresh approach was essential to prevent further failure in the transition stakes.

How to get transition right? The answer is simple ... consideration, consultation and collaboration

Consideration, consultation and collaboration are the keys to any effective transition between schools and key stages. We must never assume, impose or patronise. Nobody likes enforced change—it is likely to be feared and resented and thus be less effective than it could or should have been. Any project should be agreed and evolve naturally out of a shared commitment and enthusiasm and belief in its benefits to our students. Once these relationships are built with our colleagues and partner schools, and trust is established, then links can be developed and expanded and the possibilities are endless.

The first step to building a successful link is to have a clear educational objective; in our par ticular case it was improving questioning skills in the classroom. Then you should invite all the headteachers of your partner schools to an inaugural meeting and try to ensure that some, or preferably all, of your own school's leadership team is in attendance. Invite any interested parties from the LEA, for example, consultants at all the key stages you are covering as their expertise and guidance is reassuring and they are invaluable when it comes to advice and the production of materials. Make sure your speakers, if you have them, are knowledgeable and vaguely entertaining; after a long and possibly stressful day at school we need to be enthused and inspired—it's no mean feat. Call me shallow, but I can be swayed by the quality of the refreshments, particularly if I haven't had time to have more than a 'cuppa soup' for lunch. The way to a tired teacher's mind is definitely through their stomach. Our kitchen staff prepared a sumptuous buffet and the head, despite the perennial budget concerns, agreed to pay for the hospitality. Money well spent I should say.

By the end of the presentations and discussion on questioning skills, it was agreed that all the cluster schools would work together to improve questioning skills in infant, junior and secondary classrooms. We needed to have a project to work on. It was pointed out that there was already transition work being done prior to the infant children moving to the junior school and the juniors moving to the secondary school, and it was sensibly suggested that rather than 'another' project we should build our work on questioning into what we had already, so it would be 'new and improved' as they say. It was the practical and sensible solution especially given that the Year 6 students had already produced a questionnaire prior to their first visit to secondary school. Too often in education we far too readily throw out what we have in order to accommodate the next 'big thing'. We also had to bear in mind that three of our partner schools were through primaries and therefore a slightly different approach was needed. As a team there was nothing we couldn't achieve if we put our collective expertise to work.

The next big step

Having got everyone to agree to a project, the next big step is keeping the momentum and enthusiasm going. Nobody likes meetings for meetings' sake as they tend to generate a great deal of talk and fine ideas which never come to fruition because everyone is far too busy having meetings. Have you ever found yourself in this vicious circle? I don't doubt you have, meetings being the scourge of modern life. Still, if a transition project is to be successful then you have to meet and talk with colleagues, as collaborative planning is essential. We began planning in September 2003 with a clear deadline of May 2004, when the new transition project would be implemented after the KS1 and KS2 SATs. We agreed to meet every four to six weeks and because our questioning project covered three key stages it was agreed to have two separate working parties, one looking at questioning in the Key Stage 1 to Key Stage 2 transition and the other at the transition between primary and secondary education. The work of the first group was infinitely harder as they had to consider the issues of transition within a school and between schools. This they tackled with considerable aplomb and they should be justifiably proud of their achievements.

Our strength as a cluster was our commitment to the project and our shared goal. We were all fired with a shared belief that this project would benefit our teaching and by extension would enhance the experience of our students, equipping them with vital skills that would allow them greater access to information and promote better understanding. Effective questioning by teachers and self questioning would give students opportunities to challenge, synthesise and analyse information, whatever their stage in education; higher order questioning would lead to higher order thinking skills too.

I don't mean to sound too evangelical but I do believe that any innovation in school should have the child at its heart. Whenever I have been depressed about the state of education, or had a problem with a particular student, it is the children who have brightened my day and have reminded me why I teach. The work is under funded, exhausting and sometimes frustrating, but when things go well and you can see the benefit to the students there is no better reward. We all shared that commitment and the goal was shared rather than imposed. These features, coupled with enthusiasm, proved to be the recipe for success.

As our project progressed there were strange and unforeseen consequences. What had started out as a means to satisfy the demands of Ofsted and to get the schools in our cluster working effectively together, had turned into something we had never anticipated at the inception. We, in our East Riding backwater, had come up with a completely revolutionary way to look at tran sition. Apparently, most transition projects are just that—discrete units of work based upon a theme. What we were doing was quite revolutionary. Not only was it the only transition project to cover three key stages of education, but it was pedagogical rather than thematic.

I hadn't even given this a thought when I first planned for all the schools to meet; this was a project born out of need rather than a theory. Call me naive, but I have to confess I had never realised this (I blame my teachers, of course). Pedagogy has always existed, but have you noticed that lately it seems to have become one of those 'in' words—a name for what we practitioners hav ing been doing all along without even realising it, which is probably why this element of our work had not even crossed my mind. The beauty of a pedagogical approach is that it can be adapted to any current project and because you are teaching skills rather than working on a theme it can be adapted to any school situation. This is particularly helpful for those primary schools whose students go to several different secondary schools and who rightly say they could not possibly cover all the different transition projects. A pedagogical approach can provide the answer.

The end of the road ...?

This year marks the fourth year of the implementation of the transition project in our schools. The project is ever evolving and under evaluation. This term my new second in department and I are going to review the original scheme of work in Year 7, where we use questioning skills to enable students to write the ubiquitous autobiography, interrogate a text and finally produce a prospectus answering the sort of questions a Year 6 student may have about their new school. We now have now a clear idea of what works well and what needs to be either omitted or refined. Last October we asked the students what they enjoyed and had learned from the transition unit through the medium of our own questionnaire. The students then used this analysis and their new found knowledge to produce a group presentation. Two of these groups, comprising stu dents from all the partner schools, then had the daunting task of delivering their presentation to an assembly of their former teachers, head teachers and LEA literacy consultants. It was very enlightening, as you can imagine.

We, as secondary teachers, believe that the work in infant and primary areas has been particularly strong and that is due in part to the quality of the planning and also the fact that our primary col leagues perhaps have a clearer view of the learning process, whereas we in secondary schools have traditionally been more subject orientated and we may teach well in excess of 100 students in the course of a week. This is not meant to be a criticism of my secondary colleagues, but it is a fact. I am frankly terrified when I see the thoroughness of my sister's Year 6 lesson plans. There must be some halfway house between these key stages. Perhaps it is already a work in transi tion, if you'll pardon the pun.

The benefits of implementing successful links with our infant and primary partners have been enormous. It has been great fun, barriers have been broken down and we have learned a great deal from each other. Every year a member of the English department visits their designated partner primary to plan and team teach a transition lesson on questioning of the primary teacher's choice. This is great fun, but more importantly we have learned a great deal about the atmosphere and ethos of our primary schools as a result. We always return to our school really invigorated, usually asking questions like: 'Why aren't our students as enthusiastic as that?' or more frequently, 'What happens to students between leaving primary or junior school and coming to us in September?' These are questions that this book is seeking to address, and here in Market Weighton we are actively trying to find the answers. It is an ongoing process.

The project has not always run smoothly; things never do when you are dealing with human beings, not automata. We have had our fair share of minor problems, usually caused by a failure of communication or, more usually, technical equipment. How difficult can it be to record a question and answer session? Well sometimes more difficult than you would ever believe. Photographs and videos can also prove problematic. One year we thought we had everything covered and we had sought permission from parents and carers, but omitted to ask all the members of the panel of adults being interviewed whether they minded being recorded. We made a silly assumption, and we have never assumed since. Consideration, consultation and collaboration remain the vital tools to success at whatever level.

Funding

If you are thinking of setting up collaborative project, then funding is always an issue. Who will pay for what when budgets are often so tightly stretched? My advice is to look for any LEA or other schemes. We were lucky that our local authority was running a Leading Professionals Award Scheme at the time we were beginning our work on questioning. We had to bid for the award and funding and, with the advice and support of the KS2 and KS3 literacy consultants, the Market Weighton School English department was successful in achieving this status, two years running. The cluster therefore had £3,000 allocated to the project, with which we bought supply cover, a range of audio visual equipment to be jointly used between the schools and we were able to donate money for library books in all our partner infant, primary and junior schools. There is money out there to support such projects and I would advise you to contact your local authority in the first instance. If they are not running a scheme themselves they should be able to point you in the right direction. If you cannot source funding do not despair—good will and a sound educational idea will still get the desired result. An effective question costs nothing, and the results can be priceless.

The importance of questioning

If you would like to emulate our project, I would suggest an analysis of questioning techniques is an excellent route to begin. The following questions could be set to all parties hoping to work together.

How effective are your own questioning skills?

- Do I tend to ask closed questions, which are simply asking students to recount what they have read or learned?
- Are my questions limiting the students' responses?

- Do my questions require students to analyse a situation and apply previous knowledge or skills?
- How long do I wait for students to respond to my questions?
- On how many occasions during a lesson do I find myself answering the question myself?
- Are the same few students, the eager and focused or the more confident ones, answering all the questions whilst the remaining two thirds of the students sit mute?
- Do I ask a question and then ask students to try and work the answer out together before asking for a response?
- What is the quality of my own students' questions? Do they ask supplementary questions in order to seek further clarification?
- Do I talk too much?

I guarantee an excellent, hopefully productive discussion will follow this task. Once a common need is identified the future relationship between the schools is likely to be that much stronger.

Full details of the materials used for the questioning techniques and the relevant research used are available from Market Weighton School.

Is questioning the answer?

Finally, I will take you back to the 2002 Ofsted inspection of Market Weighton Infant School that marked the start of this transitional journey, when the quality of classroom questioning was high lighted as an area for improvement. In January 2007 the school was inspected once again and I will take the liberty of quoting from their highly complimentary report:

> The school has responded well to issues from the previous inspection, encouraging inde pendence in learning, use of questioning skills and promoting opportunities for pupils to develop their speaking skills. Questioning is used effectively to monitor pupils' progress during lessons.

> (Ofsted Inspection Report Market Weighton Infant School, 17–18 January 2007)

Far be it for me to allow Ofsted the last word, but what I would like to say is that by asking probing questions, approaching the right people and listening to their answers, transition is a positive and worthwhile experience for all involved and is 'not just for the summer term but for life'. Through consideration, consultation and collaboration, the 'three Cs of transition', we in the Market Weighton cluster have created a transition process that is firmly embedded in the teaching and learning of all our schools and it has been our privilege to share our experience with you.

I will give the final word to Rosalene Glickman (available on www.optimalthinking.com/Questions. shtml), whose words of wisdom I heard one morning on Radio 4 when I was getting ready to speak on the importance of effective questioning in the classroom one training day. It was one of those spooky moments that occur in life when you suddenly get the answer you have been looking for at just the apposite moment. Over the airwaves the speaker uttered the following thought provoking statement: 'The quality of life you have is based upon the quality of the questions you ask.'

How wise that speaker was. The statement could equally have read, 'The quality of transition is based upon the quality of the questions you ask,' as what is life, if not a journey of discovery and transition? We, as teachers, governors and parents, have a duty to assist our young people on that incredible journey through ensuring effective transition at each stage of our children's educa tional voyage of discovery. Is it to be or not to be? Indeed, 'that' is the question.

Case study 4

I have been heartened by the range of people offering case studies for this book. The ones included are by no means all of them. I was keen to find varied examples and then to allow the person describing it the space to describe the process in some detail. I hope that not only the issue they focus on, but the approaches they have used prove helpful in developing your own strategy. This one is by an old friend of mine Dave McMullan, now Deputy Head of Longcroft School. Dave never does anything without careful consideration and here describes a systematic approach to transition adopted at his popular secondary school in Beverley, East Yorkshire.

Accelerated learning
by Dave McMullan

> *The real voyage of discovery consists not in the seeking of new landscapes but in having new eyes.*

> Marcel Proust

Transition is a process often talked about with great passion and energy and yet it is often a process which is confined to the collection of data and the occasional joint INSET day between primary partners and the secondary school. Although the collection of data is more detailed these days, it so often becomes an administrative process which can easily become lost in mark books, data bases and perhaps only pedagogically active in the workings of a few teachers in the secondary school.

So what is the difference from 10 or 20 years ago? Has the process of transition moved on in this modern educational world? Is the educational process still divided by phases, potential barriers to progress and does the very idea of lifelong learning never get much beyond the very proc esses designed to encourage and nurture such an ideal?

In this case study I have attempted to describe the ways in which one school has tried to address the whole issue of transition. A school of 1,550 students with a split site and up to nine primary partners does present a logistical challenge in terms of transition; nevertheless, I believe we have made significant gains which may be of interest to other schools.

Several years ago the school recognised the need to build significant and sustainable links with its primary partners. The core subjects provided a suitable vehicle for the planning and delivery of bridging units. However, one of the most important aspects of transition is the pastoral dimen sion. It is here that I shall attempt to describe some of the processes which have taken the school from dealing with a list of student names into providing a structure which recognises each indi vidual.

Before Easter the special educational needs coordinator, working with each primary partner, will identify the most vulnerable students and begin to build a comprehensive picture of needs. With the Every Child Matters agenda uppermost in our minds the assistant headteacher will see every child and their respective class teachers; the purpose is to make contact with students and give reassurances. There is a common transfer form which contains agreed information between the two other secondary schools and all the primary partners involved. There is the electronic trans fer of all data with results and important information collated before students start; these are then issued to all staff for analysis and for the purposes of timetabling. In the autumn term of each year senior staff, which includes the head of lower school, will see all students to discuss the second ary school experience and our expectations.

Importantly, this includes a student's perspective of the new school prior to an open evening. In the summer term the year leader issues a transfer diary so that students can produce written experiences from the primary phase through to KS4. This gives valuable insight for the tutors and year leader.

In order to introduce students to the secondary school site the school makes use of a Mini Olympics tournament during the summer term. Using senior students in the school who are working towards their Sports Leadership Award, games and competitions are organised in conjunction with, and working alongside, primary colleagues. Joint drama, dance and music events are also planned in a comprehensive programme culminating in various showcase events. Again, primary colleagues work alongside secondary and with members of the local community. Resident artists and local festivals, such as the Folk Festival, are all exploited to form an enrich ment bridge between the primary and secondary phases.

Both primary and secondary staff are regularly seen on site sharing expertise on such matters as differentiation, subject specific pedagogy and behavioural strategies. This often leads to joint planning and team teaching events. One such example includes regular Modern Foreign Language sessions in which secondary colleagues are timetabled to work alongside primary col leagues in the planning and delivery of lessons. Staff quickly become regular visitors and naturally recognised when students transfer between stages.

Joint meetings are a key feature between primary schools and the secondary and engage a range of colleagues from subject leaders, key stage coordinators and senior staff. In addition, attendance officers and pastoral managers have a role to ensure that information and planning flows smoothly between primary and secondary. This allows us to plan strategically for transi tion and will include induction days and parental information events. One of the most enjoyable events is a visit to a local outward bound school where tutor groups are given problem solving activities as a way of building teams and friendship groups. The aim is to gel nine tutor groups as quickly as possible so that effective relationships are formed and learning can begin as quickly as possible.

In terms of curriculum development there have been significant changes recently which attempt to build effectively on the primary experiences. Accelerated Learning work has involved the school in working to build on the developments in one of the main partner schools. Colleagues have visited the primary school and been impressed with the quality of learning experiences and have developed through a Lead Leaner's group INSET aimed at transforming learning throughout the secondary school.

Using the same lesson plan format as in the primary school we have constructed Accelerated Learning lessons and bridging units which bring a relevance and continuity to transition. Bridging units exist in Science, Maths and English and engage staff to teach in the primary schools dur ing the summer term so that lessons can be developed further in the secondary school during the autumn term. In Science the chosen topic is bread making and follows the University of York scheme, in Maths it is numbers and their relationships, and in English the primary schools work with the secondary school on an agreed text. I shall describe the latter processes involved as it provides the generic framework for all the other bridging units.

Several years ago the school recognised the need to build significant and sustainable links with its primary partners. The core subjects provided a suitable vehicle for the planning and delivery of bridging units. It was decided to make literacy the emphasis. Literacy takes many forms and can be developed through all subjects and therefore everyone can make a significant contribution.

We invested considerable time in setting up the necessary channels for effective transition which now permeate all primary schools and the secondary school. Using local authority consultants and a cross curricular group of teachers, a new policy was devised and communicated effectively to all colleagues in the secondary phase. The policy ensured that common approaches were built on the basis of joint planning between the various schools. What follows gives a flavour of the detail and concerted efforts made to build the necessary links and the benefit afforded by careful collaboration.

Firstly, a chair of the English transition group for the consortium of schools was elected. There was a view that a potential barrier might be domination by the secondary school if they were to take control of the various agendas. We avoided this mentality at all costs and time was spent developing positive relations in which no one school was overly prescriptive or less than involved in the joint planning. The aim of transition is to ameliorate the experience of becoming attached to the senior school. As all primary schools are involved in doing the same kind of work as the secondary school, so there is a common bond and a desire to see a smooth transition between the two phases. It is this common bond which helped to guide all early discussions, including the bridging units, which were designed to begin work in the primary schools and for this work to then transfer with the student into the secondary phase.

Communication across the schools through the bridging unit means that a common dialogue develops and this extended quickly into the secondary school through such subjects as Science, Maths and Drama. Secondary tutors in the lower school soon began working with the literacy coordinator on a variety of training days to establish the nature of the bridging units, their intended outcomes and how they as tutors could work with the new students. This begins each year with tutors teaching new students on an induction day in June. Students are encouraged into mixed groups so that there is good social interaction. Each student will undertake, for example, drama through the literacy unit which has been started previously in the primary schools.

The planning groups identified four distinct phases with each building on the work of the previous one.

Stage 1

Stage 1 takes place in all primary schools, where they introduce and teach the agreed bridging text which is *Cal's Log* by Anthony Masters. All are expected to produce work for the activities in Stage 2

Stage 2

Stage 2 culminates in displays of work ready for the induction evening during the summer term in the secondary school when parents and Y6 transferring students can discuss the induction day and their work in the primary lessons. Parents of students can then view their work with the new secondary tutors. During the induction day and evening there is a celebration of the work including a video diary, displays on the night and use of the school's website to display the various activities during the day. Governors are involved and have the opportunity to meet with new students and their parents. Librarians are also present on the evening and sell dictionaries and equipment and offer advice on the library to students and parents. The evenings are always posi tive and have a relaxed atmosphere which we believe helps students and parents to feel sup ported and welcomed.

Our work on Accelerated Learning allows for a range of learning and teaching approaches in which during the bridging unit work students experience poetry, creative and persuasive writing. As an 11–18 school we benefit from involving sixth formers in the transition process. Not only do they act as excellent role models but they can use their acquired skills to help teach and support students throughout the unit work.

Stage 3

Back in the primary schools after Stage 2, the aim is to produce a board game based on the text *Cal's Log*. The students make up the rules and then produce the board game in their classes, where they then play each game and evaluate their strengths and weaknesses. The Gifted stu dents use ICT and interactive whiteboards for the same tasks. This does encourage many skills such as interpersonal, team work, self evaluation and the kind of skills that apply to just about any subject one cares to mention.

In late June, former pupils from the various primary schools will accompany the secondary teach ers to help deliver lessons and talk to students about any concerns they may have regarding the transition and to dispel the myths and legends so often associated with 'the big school'. The schools produce a travel pack for transferring students which they can take away and work on at home during the summer holidays or even in the car on holiday! The pack includes puzzles and tasks relating to literacy and the text taught. These prove to be surprisingly popular and a talking point for the very first tutor lesson with their new tutors.

Stage 4

During the first term in the secondary school, tutors and teachers of English view the methods created by the author of *Cal's Log* and how he helps to gain the attention of the reader and sets the various scenes. It connects to the work done in the primaries but is not a revisit which may lead to boredom. There is no formal assessment of the work done in the bridging units as they have recently completed the Key Stage 2 National Curriculum Assessments and will be complet ing CAT tests during the autumn term. Our aim is to have creative happy youngsters who are keen to please and enjoy their subjects.

The choice of chair for all the bridging units proved to be crucial. In all cases they had common characteristics in that they were open, friendly and had no preconceived ideas. There was no dictate and without question it had the support of all headteachers. All meetings had a clear focus for all agendas; personal communication is by phone, letter and email. The local author ity is involved in any queries and works with all colleagues to secure good planning and training through careful use of the standards fund.

Continuing to build on the primary experience

The decision was taken to introduce Accelerated Learning into the planning of lessons in a regu lar and consistent way across all subjects. Shortly after the decision was taken the local authority instigated INSET for interested schools in both the primary and secondary phases. This provided

an ideal opportunity for the school to sit down with major primary partners and establish a con
sistent format.

One of our major partner schools embraced the whole idea of Accelerated Learning and visits
to the school by Lead Learners from the secondary school was enlightening, but above all it
provided a way in which we could build effectively, so that lessons and lesson structures had
common features and a language which was to become familiar and relevant to all students.
Indeed the lesson planning used across the secondary school for the delivery of Accelerated
Learning was developed in the primary school and proved to be easy to transfer into the second
ary school.

As a result students are comfortable discussing their preferred learning styles with a wide range
of audiences and within a variety of different contexts. Lessons in both the primary and second
ary school work as one to ensure that a range of visual, auditory and kinaesthetic opportunities
are afforded. Collaboration is not just about the planning of lessons and curriculum debate; it is
also about the primary and secondary being involved in celebrating student achievement in its
widest sense. These include, for example, joint planning of various award days. Above all it's
about effective communication and positive relationships between students, staff and parents.

A Lead Learners group was established in the secondary school and one of its purposes was
to build on the primary experiences by forging a link between the primaries and the secondary
school. Some of this work involved Accelerated Learning whilst other aspects concentrated
on working with primary colleagues and developing expertise in the areas of drama, dance
and music. Show piece events are then planned and performed in the secondary and primary
schools for parents, students and members of the local community. Coaching occurs for staff
who are involved in the delivery of lessons and this extends into the secondary school as part of
the Accelerated Learning programme. This generates a feeling of continuity and involvement in
terms of curriculum delivery and the way in which the various staff teams plan.

Through this method any secondary school can work with its primary partners and the vehicle for
delivery can be whatever is pertinent to the schools involved and their community. For instance
this could be literacy, a skills based curriculum, Every Child Matters or personalised learning.

With the new Key Stage 3 curriculum shortly to be introduced there is a much greater emphasis
on the skills that students need in order to become flexible learners and to become employable
in a rapidly changing world. This could provide a suitable development that unites primary and
secondary school planning with the range of identified skills being developed in a coherent and
planned way.

In addition the new Key Stage 3 curriculum encourages not only a greater development of skills
but a more flexible approach which builds effectively on the primary experience. In this respect
the school has developed three routes for those students joining in Year 7. Not only does this
help to meet the personalised learning agenda but it allows students to work at a pace and depth
which is best suited to their needs. This is restricted to the core subjects, including Modern
Foreign Languages; however, mixed ability classes exist in all the foundation subjects. In this way
it avoids creating what is essentially a return to streaming and avoids the possible tag of social
engineering. The Gifted students are taught in the Pathfinders group; those on target to reach the
average national levels in the core subjects are placed in the Achievers group, with those who
are finding the core subjects a challenge are placed in the Springboard group. With a blocking
timetable it is possible for students to move in and out of the various groups as they progress

through the key stage. In effect, a detailed analysis is made of data and primary class teacher remarks before the various groups are established.

For so long we have talked about transition in terms of movement from the primary to the sec ondary school, but in reality every year should be viewed as a transition. Young minds change rapidly and there has to be sufficient flexibility to allow for this in a planned way. We believe that many students transferring to the secondary school, provided there has been skilled joint planning from the primary to secondary school, are capable of taking the National Curriculum Assessments at the end of Year 8. This leaves a flexible Year 9 when students can progress to GCSE early or perhaps have a broadening year when they can experience such subjects as criti cal thinking, philosophy, astronomy, the Duke of Edinburgh Award, enterprise, archaeology and the RSA programme Opening Doors. The core and foundation subjects can work in concert with each other to deliver this flexible approach, with emphasis on the delivery of skills and building on the work of the best practices experienced in many primary schools. Those who need consolida tion time can continue and take the National Curriculum Assessments in Year 9 whilst experienc ing some of the flexible approaches listed above.

In conclusion there is no doubt that this is an exciting time for curriculum development in the secondary school, when at last we are being encouraged to build on the practices of the best primary schools. If we are to take this opportunity, then secondary schools need look no further than their own primary partners, and with skilled joint planning in all key stages we have an opportunity to make the year on yearprocess of education from ages 3 to 19 a seamless and exciting one.

I hope that Dave McMullan's case study acts as a suitable aide-memoir for anyone want- ing to move their work on in a strong and sustainable way. He does not describe radical, immediate system change, but realistic change, focusing on involving all parties.

Case study 5

The next example focuses on a school very used to system change, the Sutton Centre Community School in Nottinghamshire. The school is situated in the heart of the local community, co-located with health and social services. The community and the school are inseparable, so it is not surprising that the staff have recognised that perhaps the best route to successful transition is through the parents.

The Family Homework Scheme
by Linda Orchard

The Family Homework Scheme was written with the aim of helping parents of children in Years 5 and 7, who did not wish to attend a full college based course, to develop their parenting skills. The idea was that this voluntary scheme would encourage a larger number of parents to engage in their children's education because they could take part in their learning by working with them on the activity sheets at home.

Worksheets were written aimed at helping parents and children work together to develop a range of cognitive and social/behavioural skills. Activities were devised that mirrored aspects of the Effective Parenting course, such as active listening or helping children develop a sense of responsibility by making choices and facing consequences. Support for reading, spelling and numbers was also covered. There were 12 worksheets for the Year 5 scheme and 10 for the Year 7 scheme. The worksheets were written initially for children of intellectual ability ranging from average to below average, but a differentiated scheme was introduced in 2006 to cater for all children in Year 7, from the least to the most able. Examples of the worksheets are provided free of charge online www.droppingthebaton.com. The first, entitled 'Getting to school on time', is from the Year 5 scheme; the second, entitled 'How steady is your hand?' is from the Year 7 scheme.

To help families feel that the worksheets were relevant to them the sheets were illustrated with photographs taken in the locality. To make them appear interesting and attractive they were reproduced in colour. Small incentives were distributed at intervals during the programme, such as pens and crayons. End of schemegift vouchers of £5 per child were presented at ceremonies to which participating families were invited. During 2004–05, around 200 families in Years 5 and 7 were involved, in 2005–06, around 300 and there are currently around 425. Teaching assistants at each school were paid for two hours a week to administer the scheme and a part time (one day a week) family homework coordinator, based at the college, was appointed to organise the distribution of sheets and prizes to the different schools.

In the schools where the scheme has been most effective, additional support was given, some times by learning mentors, so that the most vulnerable children were motivated to take part and achieve. The certificate ceremonies provided opportunities for a member of the Leading Edge team and the family homework coordinator, to run one off parenting workshops on activities such as the use of number lines. The former also gave information about other starter courses, such as Early Start and Keeping up with the Children.

With encouragement from local education authorities and Ofsted, and appropriate financial sup port to cover the cost of photocopying, administration and prizes, as well as a dynamic approach from those distributing and collecting the worksheets, the scheme has the potential to engage the most vulnerable families in the learning process. This might involve simplifying the Year 5 worksheets to encourage the least intellectually able children to take part.

Evaluation

Questionnaire evidence provided by 19 respondents, gathered at the end of the pilot year 2003–04 was used to evaluate the effectiveness of the Family Homework Scheme.

The aims of the pilot evaluation were to investigate the extent to which the Family Homework Scheme encouraged families to become and remain engaged and to examine the ways in which they benefited. Extracts from the evidence are given below.

Asked whether they and their children had enjoyed completing the sheets, parents said:

'Yes! She really focused on all the questions and tasks.'

'C seemed keener to do his homework if I had to help him. He enjoyed all these sheets.'

'Yes I got to spend time with her and working out the questions. It was fun.'

'You also learn with the children things you might not have known before.'

104

Asked whether they and their children had benefited, parents said:

'E has enjoyed doing the sheets so it has helped her reading and spelling.'

'Writing has improved.'

'It has helped her understand how things work.'

'It made him actually do homework rather than leaving it.'

The small scale pilot study gave some initial insights into how comparatively well motivated families responded. A full evaluation could provide valuable information on why certain families did not engage with the scheme and a route for investigating ways of overcoming their reluctance.

From a transition view point I think the above case study provides some interesting ideas. The one common thread for many pupils as they move from primary to secondary school is their home life. If the family is involved in the process of transition this surely must improve the chances of success. Primary school, secondary school and family is one threesome that might be successful!

Case study 6

When looking for a theme on which to focus transition, that of data must surely be one we can all see the potential of. In this case study two key staff from Serlby Park, Gary Bott the Vice-Principal (Primary) and Phil Palmer (Data Manager), consider how quality data can be used as the background to well coordinated educational progression.

The use and abuse of data
by Gary Bott and Phil Palmer

The traditional and well understood model on the subject of data is that it is captured, recorded, stored and transferred on request. Data is predominantly the allocation of numerical value to pupil performance. How reliable the value is depends on well tested and tried arguments concerning test validity and sample integrity. Such arguments are not usually the province of busy professionals in the classroom.

Teachers demand accurate data, well formatted data, accessible data and, crucially, data that helps them practice effectively.

Data becomes useful when it impacts on pupil performance to drive up standards. It has the potential to trigger new ways of organising pupils, new ways of interpreting progress and of describing milestones for children to achieve over time. Recent innovations in technology, for example, information management systems like SIMS, offer us an opportunity to do all of the above from age 3–18. Busy teachers are used to capturing and recording data in mark books or on sheets of paper that accumulate in pupils' folders or in the filing cabinets of heads of year. The phrase 'data rich and information poor' warns us of the danger of accepting conventional ways of measuring our pupils and valuing those measurements differentially to promote or limit opportunity. It warns against keeping track of our pupils without interrogating the reasons why.

Purposeless data collection is neither wanted nor intelligent in a thinking school. Our aim is to present the argument for data reduction here that allows for easy but effective interrogation of information to inform teachers on issues to do with target group organisation, year group organisation or even cross year group organisation.

Data is purposeful when it is meaningful and achieves clarity for the teacher in charge or the head of year to better inform decision making. Recent DfES briefings reinforce the need for effective data systems to be in place and used to support learning, inform learning and ultimately, raise attainment. Currently, data sets available to most organisations are a combination of the informal and formal, formative and summative and, occasionally, diagnostic kind. Serlby Park uses the following familiar measuring devices as a basis for our data sets: National Foundation for Educational Research (NFER), Standard Attainment Tests (SATs), optional SATs, IQ and reading results. Our view is that, though well intentioned, there is often too much information, the information is hard to interpret, teachers are trained to teach not look at numbers, and information is used too late and/or is open to misinterpretation. Intelligent schools seek information that accurately assesses attainment levels in formats that are accessible and informative at the right time for the right reasons.

The system developed anticipates RaiseOnline (formerly PAT Tracker) and was developed as a result of collaboration between primary and secondary phase colleagues that would help us work more effectively. Traditionally the problem with data documents, such as the PANDA, show school attainment and trends as numerical values represented as tables and charts. The analysis opportunity is reactive and retrospective, i.e. often the data is not available until it is too late to do anything about it or it is transferred into another phase where it is not interrogated. Systems such as RaiseOnline/PAT Tracker have the facility to target sets with some accuracy and Fast Fourier Transform (FFT) data can supplement this process. However, these offer end of key stage target values but do not give periodic milestones of how to achieve the end value.

The Serlby Park model offers a way of tracking pupil progress through milestones of achievement towards an aspiration end point value. The aspirational end of key stage target is determined from each pupil's prior attainment at KS1 through to KS2, KS3 and KS4, taking into account national average data. This model offers a way of predicting individual, group and year group performance against a hypothetical model of expected pupil progress, which we like to call a 'trajectory profile'. The obvious benefits are in checking pupil progress against conveniently placed milestones through the years and using them as aspirational targets. As the pupils make progress towards their milestones we will be able to check on their appropriateness as realistic targets for our cohorts. This should indicate when a pupil's progress is stalling and also inform decisions as to which individuals, groups or year groups need extra support.

In a 3–18 learning organisation, transition across years and key stages should not present the same kind of difficulties that occur in single phase schools. Unfortunately, it does, due to the prevailing cultures and expectations of each of the phases. One unifying thread through or in an all through school, could be a consistent system of data capture, recording and analysis that would be pertinent to Year 2 or Year 3 teachers, Year 6 or Year 7 teachers. Problems with slip page between Years 2 to 3 and Years 6 to 7 could be lessened if data and its management were managed intelligently.

What could a new model look like?

We set out on our quest by asking simple questions. Could we construct a consistent and reliable data set based on results achieved as children pass through their representative year groups? Could we formulate a mathematical model that could highlight stalling pupil progress as they achieve through the terms and years of primary and secondary school? Could SIMS, as a new technology, and particularly Assessment Manager, provide an operational response that all teachers could access easily? Could we construct a system of data collection that would build into a profile of attainment for individuals, target groups, class groups, year groups, over academic years and so track and monitor pupil progress effectively? Could we use this data to support effective individual support and guidance programmes?

To this end the vice principal, primary, and the data manager undertook the development of a new model of capturing, recording and using data to accurately track attainment and inform decisions on target groupings to sustain or accelerate progress. A dialogue ensued and further questions arose. What could it offer to teachers, parents and pupils? What could it do better than before? How would it stimulate re thinking the processes of tracking pupil progress and the set ting of milestones in the core curriculum subjects?

How does our system work?

In order to design a new target setting and tracking system, we felt it important to base it on the very system by which schools are judged, the Contextual Value Added (CVA) model. This was seen as being important for two reasons: that it would maximise the chance of the school being a success in the league tables; and more importantly it would ensure that we were build ing a system in which every child matters, rather than just the C/D borderline pupils or key stage equivalents.

We have developed, and we are continuing to improve, a system that will track pupil progress and present milestone based on Value Added (VA) data. As alluded to above, the reason for using VA data is because schools are judged by Ofsted, DfES and local authorities on CVA data. It therefore makes sense to ensure that any target setting and tracking uses a similar system. The CVA score was designed to ensure that schools focus attention on the progression of individual pupils rather than just concentrating on cohorts. It is a situation where less emphasis is given to headline figures but where the progression of all pupils is key. In fact, ensuring all pupils achieve their potential will result in an improvement in headline figures because overall standards will improve.

Why are VA targets good aspirational targets at Serlby Park?

At Serlby Park, our pupils generally enter school operating at levels below average attainment for their age group; there is a greater percentage of free school meals (FSM) and special education needs (SEN) above the national average; generally our pupils come from areas of disadvantage as measured by the local authority's multiple index of deprivation and as a result our CVA pupil targets are lower than our VA. This makes the VA model advantageous for setting our aspirational targets. For schools that are in a different circumstance, VA targets can be used to start the proc ess, however, they should be adjusted accordingly.

The trajectory profile

Our system uses Value Added data to predict an end of key stage target for each pupil in the core subjects. This end point is an aspirational target and is adjusted based upon the knowledge of our pupils to ensure that all pupils are stretched. Pupils are assessed in each subject on entry to Key Stage 2 to ascertain their starting point. With a defined starting and ending point, a line can be drawn to connect the two values, showing the expected progress of this child through KS2, which we describe as the trajectory profile.

The trajectory profile can be mathematically split into four showing the expected progress of the pupil in each year through the junior phase. Clearly, pupil progress may not follow a straight line trajectory. The yearly milestone values allow teachers to have another view of pupil progress. This can inform decisions about when interventions occur to help prevent stalling. Pupils can be split into target groups based on their yearly milestones and it will allow teachers to more effectively target resources to groups. Pupils surpassing milestones can be promoted into the next target group or even into a higher year group. There is the potential to increase targets for the pupils that surpass milestones to ensure that pupils are constantly stretched. Our view is the targets should not be reduced except for very extreme cases, necessitating input from key practitioners.

How is the KS2 trajectory profile calculated?

The VA targets, whether KS1 to KS2 or KS2 to KS4, are calculated by the DfES from national averages and show the progression of the average pupil. The Contextual VA model takes into account a pupil's background and adjusts these targets according to a variety of factors (FSM, School Prior Attainments, SEN, Deprivation Score, etc). The CVA model is therefore a much fairer system for judging a school's success because it is designed to show the expected progress of individual pupils compared to similar pupils on a national picture.

Key stage results are displayed as national curriculum levels and the DfES has assigned a certain number of points to each level with 6 points between each level. We have refined this further such that every sub level is 2 points. Average KS1 points translate to average KS2 points based on the DfES tables. We then convert these points back into levels and assign them to English, Maths and Science based on their KS1 attainment, generally at Serlby Park in the order of difficulty: English, Maths, Science.

For example:

A pupil scoring   En R 2c (13 points)
                          En W 2c (13 points)
                          Ma 2b (15 points)
                          Average = 13.6 points

On the DfES table 13.6 KS1 points should equate to 25 KS2 points, which is equivalent to two Level 4s and a Level 3. We would set targets for this pupil as a Level 3 in English and a Level 4 in Maths and Science.

The pupils are assessed on entry to Year 3 and these levels are used as a starting point. The points difference between starting assessment and KS2 target are multiplied by 0.25, 0.5 or 0.75 (Year 3, Year 4, or Year 5), added onto the starting points then converted back to a level, to give the yearly milestones. In our example above, that pupil would need to convert their English from a

Level 2c to a Level 3 by the end of KS2. That pupil may be assessed as a 1a in September (due to slippage) and would therefore be set milestones of one sub level per year.

The rationale: teachers need to be convinced that recording information on pupils will be of ben efit to what and how they teach. All data collection and use of data must be driven by the twin virtues of relevance and effectiveness. The approach taken at Serlby Park has raised teacher awareness as to the power of information. It has stimulated team approaches to target grouping and the planning of curricula to accelerate learning. The individual teacher mark sheets reflect past attainment values but also incorporate predicted outcomes for all pupils. The predicted out comes approach which underpins the use of data at Serlby Park has informed the construction of a new tracking sheet across the primary phase that will build successfully into Years 7 and 8.

Transition, slippage and grading performance

It is a well documented fact that on entry to secondary school, pupils show a massive dip in performance. This performance drop is attributed to a number of factors: change of environment, change of teachers, change of culture, change of expectations, the fact that they move from hav ing one teacher to having over 10 different teachers, etc. Recently reviewed research suggests 30 per cent error in grading pupil performance from KS2 to KS3!

When moving to a secondary environment, which targets, sets and tracks pupils in a different way, very little data actually follows a child or even gets used at all—a wasteful and unintelligent practice.

It is mostly SAT and NFER data which is used in a secondary environment. However most sec ondary schools use data such as CATs to reassess pupils themselves on entry to KS3. Part of the problem with transition and grading anomalies arise from level descriptors that are different between primary and secondary school. For example, a Level 4 in KS3 Science involves far more elements and is particularly more challenging to achieve than a Level 4 in KS2 Science.

However, national data from KS2 goes on to predict KS3 and KS4 attainment so a new trajectory profile can be formed from KS2 data. In fact, in KS3 we use KS2, CAT and FFT data to set end of KS3 targets in all subjects. As secondary teachers teach across year groups, rather than set milestone targets, we track pupils based on whether they will/will not achieve their end of key stage targets. This reduces the chance of discrepancies between KS2 and KS3 levels because rather than ask teachers to level pupils we ask whether a pupil is on course to meet their target or not. Interventions can then be formulated at an individual level after each data collection point.

The use of a consistent target setting, data collection and tracking system in primary and secondary phase, such as that used at Serlby Park, means that information tracking a pupil's progress can be passed on to the secondary school and integrated into their systems. By having accurate history on a pupil, any stalling in Year 7 and Year 8 can be quickly picked up and recti fied. The DfES produce VA tables for all the Key Stages (1–4) so a system can be used to set end of key stage targets for all years. In fact results from KS1 can predict KS2, which in turn give a prediction for KS4 (GCSE) outcome.

In theory a Year 3 pupil could be given an expected GCSE outcome based on their KS1 results, however, we would not recommend this practice at this early stage. Although linking KS1 and KS2 directly to GCSE achievement is not recommended it is clear that ensuring pupils maintain their trajectory profile is key to preventing stalling and also maximises a pupil's chances of suc cess at GCSE.

Who needs to know?

I would suggest milestone and end of key stage targets be shared with pupils, parents, teach ers, year coordinators and senior managers. If all the key players in a pupil's school and home life are kept in the loop, there is a better chance of maximising pupil potential. Input from home cannot be underestimated. We argue that better informed parents can support and encourage their children to achieve.

Well laid out and accessible data can help parents form an accurate view of pupil progress and challenge the school to account for the effectiveness of its provision. Our ultimate aim is to ensure the school environment is one that promotes high expectations rather than settling for the satisfactory. Good data management and its use to inform teaching and learning can work towards achieving that aim.

Benefits

The benefits of our new model have been to anticipate the RaiseOnline/PAT Tracker and allow teachers to monitor and track individual, target group and year group progress through the aca demic years. The model's predictive potential to indicate exit grades for individual pupils based on their entry values is a trajectory profile or progress path. The trajectory profile is a line that describes progress based on national averages from Key Stage 1 through to Key Stage 2 and on into Key Stage 3 and 4.

The trajectory profile is based on a simplified model of numerical values attached to grades, set against national benchmarks or expectations at Key Stage 1, 2, 3 and 4. The profile is essentially predicted expectations of attainment that most children should achieve at the end of each key stage. In schools serving disadvantaged communities the milestones set between each of the key stages present aspirational targets.

The milestones are calibrated as a simple division of the number of terms divided into the points difference on entry and exit to each key stage. We fully realise that this is simplified and conven ient in terms of equal distribution. Some children will not achieve in line with their profile and oth ers will exceed this line of expectation, but these aspirational targets or milestones will be a guide in each of the year groups so teachers can judge whether a child is on target to reach their end of key stage attainment and whether the model has real value.

The trajectory profile becomes one means of informing other teachers and parents about per formance. It is an excellent reference point for parents when they ask the question, 'How good is he?' 'Is she getting on OK for her age?' It will allow accurate grouping of pupils and indicate underperforming and overachieving pupils. A note of caution here: as Serlby Park pupils grow through the system their actual performance levels will be compared to their predicted milestones and this will help us to judge the accuracy of this model in both measuring pupil progress and anticipating progress. It should provide information so there is a better match of the curriculum to pupil need. It will allow us to produce a trajectory profile comparison of expected and actual attainment levels at a pupil, group and year group level.

The trajectory profile will help year group leaders to assess the strengths and weaknesses of particular cohorts. It will identify the lowest and the highest achievers. It will allow the identification of pupils making slower than expected progress. It will allow teachers to judge whether the mile stones represent a realistic expectation of pupil performance through each of the year groups to better understand if progress is gradual or stepped or, as in transfer, slips backwards. The more we know about how pupil progress looks over an academic year and through phases, the more accurately we will be able to predict outcomes at GCSE level.

SIMS Assessment Manager is now flooded with individual teacher mark sheets which are ranged in such a way as to make comparisons of normative assessments easier. Predominantly, stand ardised scores are used in the core subjects. Options available for teachers include the ordering of pupils in a core subject in ascending or descending order of rank. It allows the quick identifica tion of percentages of the class or year group cohort expected to achieve national benchmarks at Level 4 or Level 5. It allows year groups to be compared side by side to identify the Gifted and Talented who might then be grouped together. The ease of analysis of the marksheets will better inform teachers about how, when and why they group children as they do. It will challenge cur rent ways of target grouping children as single year groups rather than double or even triple year group associations.

The interesting future for this model will be to compare it with the potential of the PAT Tracker and also the reality of pupils' actual achievement. It will allow inter and intra year group variations to be revealed to inform deployment of resources. It will address the concern about pupil progress stalling in particular year groups, traditionally thought of as soft or consolidation years. There are no soft year groups any more. Every year group has to maximise pupil progress and the mile stones trajectory profile model might help us do this.

The frequency of the sampling of pupil attainment will be fine tuned as the profile is embedded in practice. It will give rigour to teacher judgments about pupil progress and it should be easier to communicate to parents and colleagues at an individual, group and year group level. It is a tool to be used to improve teacher effectiveness and accurately track pupil progress. It will be adapted as children's real achievements begin to populate the trajectory profile tracking sheet.

The impact of the trajectory profiling at Key Stage 3 and 4, using the traffic lights system of track ing pupil progress, has effectively informed the Year 11 mentoring programme and supported mentors in mentee analysis of strengths and weaknesses.

Universal teacher access to SIMS via their desktop PC or laptop means they are connected to a database unlike any other mark book ever invented. The value of this to support teachers and pupils in their learning journeys has yet to be fully validated. Initial responses from teachers are that the mark sheets and group sheets and year group profiles have tremendous potential. The next stage will be to use them intelligently to promote improved outcomes for all.

The focus of this report is pupil attainment and is one of a raft of measures used at Serlby Park to gather information about how well pupils are doing at school. Taken together with attendance and behaviour packages already in place, issues around transition will diminish as we use data to better effect and impact on pupil progress intelligently.

So the message to us must surely be that many themes can be used as the centre for transition work: data, questioning, teaching styles and homework, to name but a few. The common thread to all of these is firstly a common need (not a perceived need by one side only), and secondly a common desire and passion to do something about it.

How do we build new ways of learning?

The revolution has started ...

This section is for those of you who have seen the light so brightly that you are almost blinded. You are probably pacing your room, crying 'yes, yes, yes' (may I suggest you close the windows before the neighbours get completely the wrong idea). You want to get really serious about transition—you want to stop tinkering at the edges of transition. This section contains real examples of system change that works:

Suzie Kent, a high-energy teacher from Serlby Park (one of the first to experience teaching on all sites of the 3–18), feels that real change will not occur unless greater numbers experience teaching across the phases.

> Cross phase teachers are able to offer comfort to pupils in transition, as they provide a familiar face and can help pupils settle in—they know which pupils will need that extra time/support because the teacher already has knowledge of family history/problems, etc. The teacher already knows the ability of the children so no new assessments are required, there is little unknown territory and pupils are aware of teacher expectations/standards, etc.
>
> How else can we overcome transition?
>
> • By making more effective use of data transfer. For example, this academic year we have moved further to improve transition by all staff having access to the sleuth system.
> • By increasing the number of transition meetings—making sure that they have a specific focus, that recommendations are actioned and information is disseminated effectively to all members of staff.
> • Increase peer lesson observations thereby raising KS2 and KS3 teachers' awareness of pupils' standards and increasing understanding about how subjects and skills are taught. Peer observations can also raise KS1 and KS2 teachers' awareness of how they can prepare pupils for KS2 and KS3'

Maybe the thought of developing teams of cross-phase teachers is a step too far for you? Help is at hand! Some excellent support is available from the RSA Opening Minds project, which is a perfect vehicle for redesigning the Year 7 curriculum. Here, one of the people behind the project, Barrie Wyse (a top class deputy head I had the privilege of working with in Hull), explains what it is all about.

Opening Minds

Opening Minds is a curriculum framework developed at the RSA. The driving force is a set of 24 competences arranged in five categories: Citizenship, Learning, Information, People, Situations—CLIPS for short. Competence is about having skills and understanding how and when to use them most effectively.

Primary schools have successfully developed Opening Minds work. In secondary schools the focus is initially on KS3.

A small group of schools piloted Opening Minds, exploring ways of developing the competences. In most cases this was done by creating modules which last half of a term or projects that incorporate material from a range of subjects, the subject range varying from school to school. Any or all subjects can be incorporated into projects, even if some of the included subjects also have discrete timetable time. Subjects 'outside' the project can make important contributions; they may have particularly relevant content or subject specific skills from which students will benefit during their work on the project.

These projects are planned by the team of teachers whose subjects contribute to the Opening Minds work. Typically, all the projects are taught in one to three hour blocks by all of the team, regardless of individual subject specialisms. On the basis of schools' experience, we recommend that Opening Minds work occupies a minimum of 30 per cent of the timetable and that whenever possible each teaching group works with one teacher in their own working space or room, although sometimes project teaching is successfully shared by two teachers.

Some schools have a lead lesson with the year group and all the Opening Minds team. Others work for longer periods with larger groups and team teach.

The set of competences from the RSA is not intended to be definitive or immutable. Schools rewrite these in language more appropriate for their students; some reduce the number by combining elements of different competences.

The curriculum framework offers students and teachers the opportunity to make the curriculum more coherent and connected. Teachers pool and share their expertise, often with surprising results; students come to a greater understanding of the links between subjects.

Schools report many benefits from the development of Opening Minds work. Teachers value:

- much greater opportunity to get to know students really well
- better working relationships
- students taking control of their own learning
- students' ability to develop language which facilitates analysis and recording of their learning
- more students completing more work to a higher standard
- significantly improved motivation and behaviour
- greater achievement across the ability range
- confidence of students to be challenging in a positive way
- working with, and support of, colleagues
- positive responses of parents and visitors
- being able to move around during lessons
- using Opening Minds teaching and learning styles in other lessons
- development of new skills and expertise
- greater understanding of the whole curriculum

Students say they value:

- not having so many teachers
- teachers who admit it when they don't know things
- having 'our own' room
- 'not having to carry stuff around all the time'
- setting own timescale
- time to complete work without being rushed

- working in groups
- being able to carry on with work during break and lunchtime
- having fun
- doing presentations to parents and others
- learning important things for life

Schools consistently report improved motivation, improved behaviour, better teacher/student, student/student working relationships and students having a greater understanding and owner ship of their learning. When schools have run control groups the difference between the out comes from pilot and control groups have been quite dramatic.

The experience of working in the Opening Minds team often results in teachers reassessing their teaching, resulting in a wider impact within the school.

A number of factors impact on transition:

- use of home base for Opening Minds work
- less movement, fewer teachers
- closer interaction with one teacher [30 per cent plus of timetable]
- Year 7 not a 'repetition' year
- possible links to partner schools also running Opening Minds
- appointment of ex primary teachers specifically to work in Year 7 with Opening Minds
- teaching and learning styles and classroom experience more closely related to primary school

Some secondary schools have successfully run 'mini' Opening Minds projects on their Year 6 induction days.

Increasingly, schools are looking at alternative ways of organising and presenting the formal cur riculum. Opening Minds offers marked improvement in transition, a more coherent curriculum and the development of a wide range of competences that are important for life both within and outside school.

To see the full list of competences and to find out more about Opening Minds and materials avail able to download or buy, go to www.thersa.org/newcurriculum.

There is no doubt that projects such as Opening Minds are beginning to force schools to break away from the restraints of old fashioned curriculum. Secondary schools must stop being sausage factories where Year 7 pupils are simply taking the first steps to fill their glistening skins! For us at Serlby Park, we decided that the issues of transition required fundamental system change—what better way to challenge thinking than to completely amalgamate an infant, junior and secondary school. Here is how it began.

Serlby Park—an all-through solution

Serlby Park has grown to become one of, if not *the*, most high profile all-through school in the country. This has happened within two years and has been done without new buildings, just great amounts of good will and energy. The key factor to success has been the early realisation that amalgamation offered improved chances for the pupils—this reason alone was the rationale for the process.

Serlby Park serves the area of Bircotes and Harworth, which is crudely referred to as one of rural deprivation. Harworth Colliery has recently been mothballed and the houses built to serve this once mighty giant have no other major local employer to turn to. The community is a hugely proud one and many individuals have used local enterprise units to start their own companies. The facilities for the community are limited and although it is in North Nottinghamshire, the area closer echoes the traditional Yorkshire pit village.

The secondary school in the area, Bircotes and Harworth Community School, was small and after a number of years of low performance and dwindling roles in the early 1990s began a revival which by 2001 saw it regularly appear in national league tables for value added. This was accompanied by a 30 per cent increase in year group size to a point where most years were full. The largest feeder primary was North Border Junior School, from which more than 70 per cent of pupils transferred. This in turn was fed by North Border Infant School. Both of these schools had high standing with parents in the community and very positive value added scores. It is important to review the facts: improving exam results, a positive relationship with the community, stable population and an established headteacher in each school. In other words there were no external pressures to amalgamate; the momentum to do so was created by the three headteachers and the local authority with a sole focus of improving learning. I am concerned when visited by delegations of staff considering a similar route to find that in some cases LAs see all-through education as a solution to budget problems or recruitment issues. These may be a happy by-product, but are weak foundations on which to build a learning community.

The setting of a core philosophy on which to focus the new project was key to its success. This meant that opposition from the community, governors, staff and unions was small, and was limited to practical issues that were often easy to address. The three governing bodies embraced the project, even though the amalgamation would remove at least two of them. For a variety of practical reasons the precise mechanism chosen in this case was to close the infant and junior schools and extend the age range of the secondary. Many would imagine that this would be a disastrous method, cementing an idea at the core of the new school that secondary education dominated and that this was effectively a 'take-over'. Identifying this potential problem meant that action could be taken to ensure that the true 'partnership of equals' nature of the project became clear to all. Hence the infant and junior governing bodies supported rather than opposed the amalgamation, with the headteachers of the two primary sections both enthusiastically promoting the benefits, even though their own roles would be dramatically altered. Gary Bott, the ex-headteacher of the infants, and now vice-principal of Serlby Park, always smiles when asked by visitors if he minded losing the sole responsibility of the infants: 'Why would I? I used to influence the education of 230 young people; I now directly shape the lives of 1,200!'

However, moving from the realisation of what we wanted, to making it happen in well under a year was a task that would send a shiver down even the stiffest spine. The temptation was to begin rapidly planning everything,

- How would we lead the school?
- How would we arrange staffing?
- How would we arrange the finances?

- What would we do to make the school all-through?
- What changes do we need to make to the buildings?
- What changes do we need for the ICT infrastructure?
- What changes do we need for the name?
- What changes do we need for the uniform?
- What changes do we need for the badges and signage?

The four senior leaders (oh, how I hate hierarchical terms!), Gary (Headteacher of Infants), Barry (Headteacher of Juniors) , Steve (Deputy Headteacher at Secondary) and myself (Headteacher of Secondary) went for an intensive two-day meeting at a local hotel to resolve the burning questions. Our guide and facilitator for the process was the charismatic consultant/author/actor and educationalist Roy Leighton who specialises in pushing people way out of their comfort zone and who startled us all by telling us we were not going to answer any of the questions from our list.

Cries of, 'We haven't got time for any trendy stuff—we've got work to do!' were on our lips, but his wisdom has benefited us greatly. By spending time developing our philosophy for the school and by getting to know each other's strengths and weaknesses, we were in a much stronger long term position than if we had pandered to our insecurities requiring us to try and dot i's and cross t's. Roy challenged us not to worry about the long term staffing structure of the school, claiming that this was 'organic'. At the time I found the term 'organic' a difficult one to accept, believing it had no place in a situation like ours. How wrong I was! But how right he was, and watching the school grow has been one of the greatest privileges of my career.

In fact from our list above the only questions we had completely answered by the time the doors of the new school opened were the last four: new ICT structure to enable improved communication between the sites, new name, uniform, badges and signs to ensure that a sense of identity and positive community was created. Some of the other questions we haven't even fully answered yet!

It is very empowering (but also frightening) to begin a new school openly saying, 'This is how we are going to start doing things, and we'll develop it as we go along.' We opened in September 2005 when the obvious changes were limited to cosmetic ones—the majority of staff were carrying out the same role in the same place. Indeed the initial leadership team was just rebadged as shown below.

Leadership structure

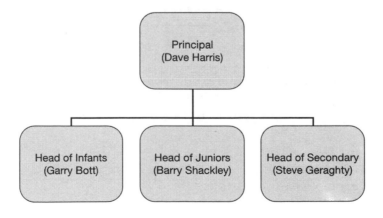

My role was to become 'strategic, financial and buildings', the other three to be the day-to-day leaders for their area. I was surprised at how straightforward this section of development was, although frequent meetings and lots of honesty were essential in avoiding major issues. The changes in nuance of each role were not of concern to most staff as the faces were initially based in the same places. This concept of gradual change becomes a key symbol of all-through education, where the whole premise of the organisation is based around reducing transition trauma, accepting that change will happen, but smoothing the process by which it occurs.

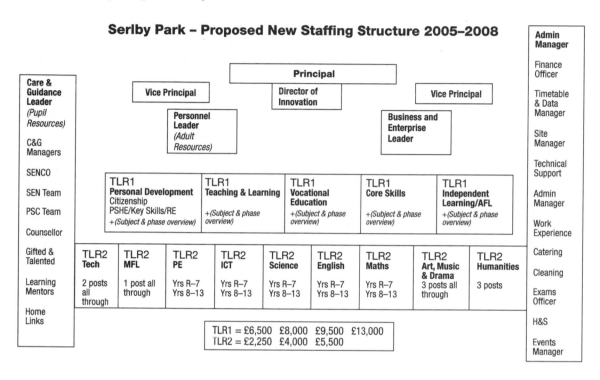

Once the new school was under way a new 'ideal' structure was developed in consultation with staff and the independent consultant Kelvin Peel. Once published this was presented as something we would gradually move towards.

A key part of this structure is the removal of subject domination in the middle levels of school leadership, very much a typical part of most secondary schools. It was quickly recognised that if an all-through structure bases its senior posts around subject specialism this structure will automatically become secondary in its nature. Also the ideal of filling leadership posts with staff from all experiences is greatly reduced as any post advertised with major subject responsibility at its core will inevitably favour candidates from secondary who have focused on the development of subject expertise within their career. Therefore the Teaching and Learning Responsibility (TLR) 1 posts we advertised were:

Personal development (PSHE, Citizenship, Health/Sex Education)
Teaching and learning (all activities relating to improved practice)
Lifelong learning (new courses/personalisation/choice)
Core skills (literacy, numeracy, key skills)
Independent thinking (developing pupils' ability to learn and motivate themselves and others)

Applicants were attracted from across all phases and were filled by high calibre enthusiastic staff from both primary and secondary backgrounds. These staff members are beginning to work very effectively as a team, leading in areas of vital importance to the development of any school, whilst also undergoing practical roles supporting the works of subject and pastoral teams.

The subjects are coordinated though TLR2s where two posts from different phases jointly discuss the development of the subject. It is important to note that neither post is senior to the other and that a single budget ensures that the individuals do talk and liaise. Also worthy of mention is that the more primary role officially has responsibility to the end of Year 7, ensuring a smoother development of subject knowledge. In some subjects, such as Art, Drama and Music, a single person coordinates the work across the whole age range.

The vertical boxes either side of the structure are mainly filled with practical roles that span the whole school. Very quickly single posts were established to coordinate catering, manage attendance and examinations. The day-to-day work of some of the care and guidance team separate into three phases but work very closely and produce all policies and procedures together.

Over two years the structure has grown from being lines and boxes on paper into a living and breathing 3D organisation. The observation of the 'real' thing quickly led to the realisation of the weakness of using the box model. This has too many links to the Victorian line management system so favoured by secondary schools, which was introduced to suit the factories of the manufacturing era. These structures are by their very nature rigid and very slow to adapt to changing environments. Our own structure above features the pyramid shape which traditionally focuses all eyes on the person at the top, who controls everything below—this must be the wrong type of image for a modern school. Change of such major proportions cannot occur from a 'top down' model, but must be initiated by the people closest to it.

This has led to a search for other, more organic, ways to represent the leadership of Serlby Park. The diagram opposite is our closest current model (though will certainly evolve further!). The spiral shows a flow through the organisation, but links roles that influence each other on either side of the line. Staff are encouraged to think of their decision-making as if the structure was a pond and the decision a stone causing ripples—they are at liberty to cause the ripples, but must consider the effect of their action on the whole pond and how it combines with the ripples from others around them.

Every day that I walk around Serlby Park I am excited by the connections being formed, resulting in some superb transition work developing. This approach is very different to the traditional headteacher model, one where everything must originate from the top. I have seen heads who are thrown into steaming fits by discovering something that they know nothing about, whereas I take it as a sign of a healthy school and good leadership.

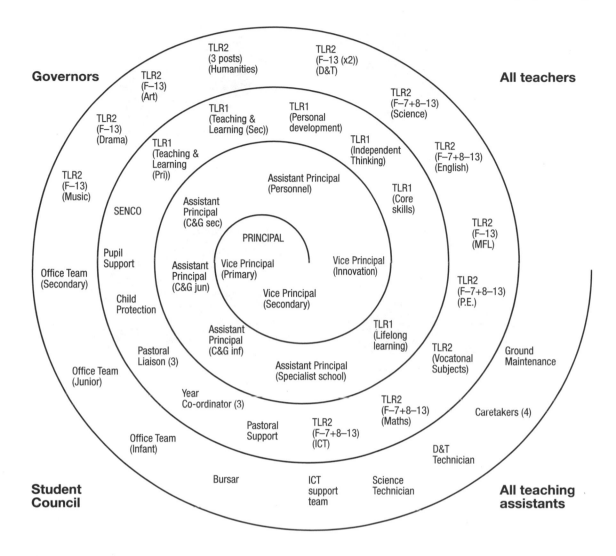

Governors

All teachers

TLR2 (3 posts) (Humanities)

TLR2 (F–13 (x2)) (D&T)

TLR2 (F–13) (Art)

TLR2 (F–7+8–13) (Science)

TLR2 (F–13) (Drama)

TLR1 (Teaching & Learning (Sec))

TLR1 (Personal development)

TLR1 (Independent Thinking)

TLR2 (F–7+8–13) (English)

TLR1 (Teaching & Learning (Pri))

TLR2 (F–13) (Music)

Assistant Principal (Personnel)

TLR1 (Core skills)

TLR2 (F–13) (MFL)

SENCO

Assistant Principal (C&G sec)

PRINCIPAL

Pupil Support

Assistant Principal (C&G jun)

Vice Principal (Primary)

Vice Principal (Innovation)

TLR2 (F–7+8–13) (P.E.)

Office Team (Secondary)

Vice Principal (Secondary)

Child Protection

Assistant Principal (C&G inf)

TLR1 (Lifelong learning)

Ground Maintenance

Office Team (Junior)

Pastoral Liaison (3)

Assistant Principal (Specialist school)

TLR2 (Vocatonal Subjects)

Year Co-ordinator (3)

TLR2 (F–7+8–13) (Maths)

Caretakers (4)

Office Team (Infant)

Pastoral Support

TLR2 (F–7+8–13) (ICT)

D&T Technician

Student Council

Bursar

ICT support team

Science Technician

All teaching assistants

I have often explained to visitors that amalgamating the three schools has been like being a gardener trying to get three bushes to grow together. Slowly the branches entwine and the gaps between them fill up. If you take a few steps back it looks like one big plant; look underneath and the three different roots are clearly seen. Every branch and leaf trying to bridge the gap must be nurtured.

Here are a few examples of branches:

Awards evening—celebrating the best scientists at each key stage. Developing a learning *community*!

Junior Sports Leaders (Year 10 with Year 6), organised by a teaching assistant—now raising their own finances and making a real *difference* to transition.

Radio station—totally run by the
pupils. Music to support learning
during lessons, approved playlist
during break

Year 10 pupils work with Year 1s
on literacy

Healthy eating tuck shop run
by the pupils—stock check,
appointments and finance all
managed by them

A mixed age group samba class—
enjoying, supporting and learning

It is interesting that opening the box of improving transition has released so many excit-ing developments. Perhaps the most exciting of these has been the formation of a com-petency curriculum for Year 7. For the first two hours each morning, all Year 7s work with their tutor on a specialised curriculum. The team is made up of secondary teachers headed by a primary colleague, Ellen Leese. Ellen is TLR1 in charge of Teaching and Learning, and a very positive force for change, and is rapidly gaining a unique insight into the issues surrounding transition. I asked Ellen to describe her experience.

The Year 7 project

'You must be absolutely barmy!' This was the initial reaction of my primary colleagues when I announced that I would be teaching at the secondary site for the first two hours of every day. The current Year 6 was a challenging group and some teachers were pleased to be sending them on their way into the secondary phase. I, on the other hand, was very eager to face a new and excit ing challenge of being part of an innovative curriculum that primarily would support transition and help the pupils to have a seamless move from one site to the other as part of the 3–18 initiative.

Starting up

The initial planning and organisation was set up by the primary head, Barry Shackley. He recruited a team of volunteers from the secondary site who were interested in giving this idea a go. So we began with a team of five, four were secondary teachers with specialisms in Maths, Art, English and MFL, whilst one was a specialist in primary education. A conscious decision was made to have all five forms being taught at the same time in order to create a unified project. It was also decided that it was very important for all five forms to be within the same block. Understandably this caused problems for the humanities team who then had to use different classrooms for the first part of the day, but unfortunately there was no other solution.

The curriculum

The teaching team were interested in learning about different subjects for their professional development and we decided to follow a project based curriculum. We looked into the RSA Opening Minds competency based curriculum but at the time it seemed too open ended and the guidelines were very broad. This decision was based only on the fact that we had very little time to plan and resource the projects, as this was researched in May 2006 with the intended implementation in September.

The International Primary Curriculum (IPC) was an 'off the peg' solution to our time constraints. It is based on clearly defined learning goals or standards which lay out the subject, personal and international knowledge, skills and understandings children need at different stages of their school life. There was a significant cost implication to using this scheme but some of the projects have been incorporated into the primary phase and at the time it offered the structure for delivery and assessment that we needed as a new team.

During the year we have added to the projects and adapted them so that they are more tailored to our needs, but overall the projects have been relevant and cross curricular which was what we wanted. The humanities team gave us a list of skills that they wanted the pupils to learn throughout this year, as History and Geography were included in the project time and not taught exclusively at any other time. This is something that is to be changed for next year, with at least one lesson of each being taught by the specialist teachers.

What has gone well?

From the beginning there were hardly any transition issues—fears and myths were dispelled during the first few days and pupils were supported in navigating the school. The forms have built up a relationship, not only with their form tutor but also with each other. This is largely due to group working but also from tackling challenges that involve communication and problem solving, which the curriculum allows. The pupils frequently work outside of the classroom in the communal corridor area, resulting in pupils from different forms working together and so developing interdependent skills. Also when drama activities have been used to present learning, pupils from other forms have watched and evaluated the performances even though they have still been at the work in progress stage.

The pupils regularly express how much they enjoy their tutor time and wish that the rest of their day was structured in the same way. There are very few negative behaviour issues during the first two periods of the day and those that do arise are quickly dealt with via a structured approach of support between the tutors. Primary practice has very much been maintained with regard to behaviour rewards. The pupils set their own class rules and asked to have 'golden time' as a reward for good behaviour/hard work. This has been respected but is carried out fortnightly and is positively reinforced. The culture of respect between form and tutor supports this and the maturity of the pupils ensures that it is not a given, which usually occurs with younger children.

The teaching team have worked really hard and are beginning to reap the rewards. All of those involved have really enjoyed the experience and want to continue next year—which speaks volumes. We have all taught in new subject areas and have risen to the challenge—not that we can't improve on some performances for next year but this is all part of professional development. We are experiencing success but are constantly evaluating and reassessing our objectives. It is important to get the pupils involved too, giving them a voice and allowing them to develop their own curriculum (e.g. What did they enjoy? What could be improved and how?). Due to its infancy this has to be a flexible process. One of the most significant comments that has been made by the team is that from their point of view they have developed a very different relationship with the pupils than they usually do over an academic year and that they feel 'protective' towards their form. This is very much a primary principle and could not be predetermined.

Even better if ...

Obviously there have been teething problems and obstacles that have had to be overcome. Finding time to meet as a team has been a problem as we all have commitments to other depart ments. However, this has to be made a priority next year. It is essential to give each other the support as well as continually evaluating the process. The IPC projects have been an excellent starting point but the planning needs to be more clearly defined with the learning objectives and assessment expectations made more explicit. There is also a need for further differentiation within the work to cater for all ability groups. The work is usually differentiated by outcome with most of the tasks being research based but a more structured approach is required for less able pupils.

Although behaviour is not an issue during tutor time, unfortunately it is during the rest of the day. This is an ongoing problem and although we have strategies for dealing with any issues the following day, a more instant response would have greater effect. To be honest, having respon sibility for a form is a two way process and as a form tutor you can be seen as accountable for the behaviour of the individuals within your form. This can be awkward at times, especially if the children are well behaved when they are with you.

I would like to make provision for more parental involvement next year. Although this is a primary practice, it is too often assumed that children instantly grow up when they reach Year 7 and this is not the case. As a primary practitioner I am aware how strongly parents rely on your support with their children and an automated cut off point should not always be enforced.

Quantative assessment is very difficult, especially if you do not specialise in the subject you are assessing, e.g. History. The Year 7 project is more about process and less about product. If a group are working on a task and the objective is to work as a team, if the end product is not of a good standard then it doesn't matter—as long as the group can evaluate where they went wrong and can build in preventative measures so that it doesn't happen again.

This being said, qualitative assessment is probably more specific and detailed. A thorough understanding of each child is acquired and this can and, more importantly, should be used to inform other teachers about each pupil.

The way ahead

This has only been an introductory year and there is a steep learning curve. We have dipped our toes into the water and now it is time to dive in. There are improvements to be made and a more rigorous approach is required, but at least this has been identified and so something will be done.

The beneficial effects on the pupils are obvious: the majority of pupils have an increased aware ness of how they learn and how to interact in a socially responsible way. We are looking to incor porate more competence based skills into the curriculum for next year and we are working with the current Year 7 to determine what important ones these are.

Once you consider removing boundaries for Year 7 pupils, you soon ask yourself if there any other changes you can make to benefit pupils across the whole age range.

Why 16, why GCSEs?
by Steve Geraghty, Vice-Principal of Serlby Park

Ever wondered why GCSEs remain so popular despite the best efforts of many educationalists to move away from them. The simple answer is that secondary timetables permit very little change and, in fact, the operation of the system is a straitjacket preventing change. The personalised learning agenda will be obstructed on many levels unless timetablers offer a modernising twenty first century vision.

Many teachers may tell you that GCSEs offer the best way to compartmentalise teaching into solid subject 'chunks', supported by examining bodies who provide great course outlines and teaching materials. Teachers will also tell you that they themselves succeeded in this system (admittedly they were probably called 'O' Levels) and hence it is a process they understand and can work within. What they will also tell you is that they do have doubts about their suitability for a great proportion of the students in their charge, but they don't really know how to move in any other direction. Well, the good news is that society will find it difficult to blame teachers for intransigence; whether alone, or in small groups, teachers can move very little because school timetabling remains firmly rooted in the past. Changing the structure of timetables will be the big gest impetus to change.

There are two basic obstacles to greater choice within any geographical area or individual institu tion, namely travel needs and institutional/subject competition. Areas vary in the needs of their students to travel. For many it is time taken from the teaching day and the escalating costs of transport are prohibitive. Where there is extensive movement, even within one school day itself, the costs in terms of time and money multiply. Competition in some geographical areas is fierce; retaining student numbers is the main priority and hence collaboration is perceived as danger ous. So too, in many schools, widening subject choice, even within departments, is seen as damaging to the status quo of subjects. The net result is inertia, conveniently supported by argu ments that the timetable won't allow this or won't allow that!

There is a conceptual impetus to change this, however, under the simplified guise of 'person alised learning', but what is obvious to most observers is that personalised learning is a distant dream unless we widen student choice and bring in other partners to offer courses which better attempt to satisfy student interests and aptitudes. Conceptual approaches are useless unless backed up by genuine logistical change. Start with the timetable.

If genuine collaboration is fully supported and operational, then the first timetable move is to create two common days throughout the geographical area (consortium). This will cut down on travel needs, monitoring students will be easier, staffing movement is aided greatly and all part ners, from the work based learning sector to the employers, to the schools and colleges, will have a recognised working template. A major school issue will be solved as students miss no other lessons from the 'core' curriculum. Undoubtedly, such a move will face opposition; it will mean Maths, English and Science lessons are condensed into fewer days and many staff desire only the one lesson a day in the same subject. It may also be unpopular with the 'option' subjects who will complain that their lessons are condensed into two days and thus possible 'overload' will result.

The happy news is that neither seems true. Research points to the brain disposing of the bulk of information which has not been reinforced within 24 hours so this system would actually enhance learning. In addition, longer learning periods have been advocated by many as benefiting the student by facilitating a greater range of teaching and learning methodologies. Modern Foreign Languages take note: you will have the time and opportunity to set up regular video conferencing links, bo inclined to purchase more Interactive software and specifically take advantage of the new opportunities that this time affords.

If the collaboration made possible by these changes is seen to be of benefit to the students in terms of increasing motivation, rising examination results and retention rates, then this should reduce institutional insecurities, combatting one of the main obstacles to innovative change.

Within schools, many subject teachers fear a widening of choice because it poses an immedi ate threat to student numbers on the 'traditional' courses. With the new timetable structure, student numbers will rise, not fall, as is feared. If days are blocked the traditional option difficul ties within years will fade away as subjects are now opened to other year groups on the blocked days. The notion that GCSEs/other qualifications should be offered only to 16 year olds is under attack from many quarters anyway, as more schools and colleges pick up qualifications earlier. What the model shows are the possibilities of timetable change: schools could block only Year 10 and 11, or alternatively, all three of the final years of secondary schooling up to 16. Possible student numbers offered option choices will be increased and so will the recruitment possibilities for subjects across the spectrum. Wanted to try BTEC but couldn't face the prospect of losing GCSE completely? Wanted to bring in a vocational qualification but could not recruit a special ist because the periods were spread throughout the week? The winner in all this is the student because personalised learning has a basis of greater choice.

The possibilities of qualifications at an earlier age have other ramifications. Does student moti vation drop the nearer they get to 16? Should they be caught when their enthusiasm levels are higher, albeit their subject capabilities are not? With regard to this latter point, is it true that attitude, and not aptitude, is the greater priority for subject success? We can also add extrinsic motivation to the debate: how can it exist in any great measure when currently the rewards for completion of a two year course come when the student has already left school? The conse quences of squeezing time for another two GCSE/equivalents out of the system by using Year 9 as a GCSE year in this way would be a subject of future research, but the advantages of having more option choice and earlier extrinsic reward cannot be easily ignored. There is never a defini tive answer to change management timings, but is it not more preferable to spot the bus before it hits you?

The future for English education is certainly intertwined with the personalised learning agenda and this time the impetus for change is undeniably unstoppable. Collaboration and innovative change lie at the very heart of this. Timetablers have the opportunity to literally move the educa tional world; it won't be easy, moving a massive weight never is, but it will be worth the effort!

Here is a practical example of how I have started to solve these issues at Serlby Park.

The Key Stage 4 timetable at Serlby Park (2007/2008)

Year Group	Monday Core	Tuesday Option	Wednesday Core	Thursday Core	Friday Option
11	Maths	PE	Maths	Maths	PE
	English	Resistant	English	English	Resistant
	PE	Materials Course	PE	PE	Materials course
	Cit/RE	French	Cit/RE	Cit/RE	French
	Science	Food	Science	Science	Food
	WRL (Work Related Learning course)	Spanish	WRL (Work Related Learning course)	WRL (Work Related Learning course)	Spanish
		Geography			Geography
		Childcare			Childcare
		Business			Business
		Construction			Construction
		History			History
		Health & Soc			Health & Soc
		Drama			Art
		CoPE (Competency based qualification)			Drama
		ICT			CoPE (Competency based qualification)
		Horse Care course			ICT
		Music			Horse Care course
		Work Placement			Music
		College Courses			Work Placement
					College Courses
10	Maths	History	Maths	Maths	Construction
	English	Health & Soc	English	English	History
	PE		PE	PE	Health & Soc
	Cit/RE	Drama	Cit/RE	Cit/RE	Art
	Science	CoPE (Competency based qualification)	Science	Science	Drama
	WRL (Work Related Learning course)	ICT	WRL (Work Related Learning course)	WRL (Work Related Learning course)	CoPE (Competency based qualification)
		Horse Care course			ICT
		Music			Horse Care course
		Work Placement			Music
		College Courses			Work Placement
					College Courses
9	Maths		Maths	Maths	
	English		English	English	
	PE		PE	PE	
	Cit/RE		Cit/RE	Cit/RE	
	Science		Science	Science	
	WRL (Work Related Learning course)		WRL (Work Related Learning course)	WRL (Work Related Learning course)	

* Example Option week

	Tues	Friday
Period 1	PE	History
Period 2	PE	History
Period 3	Drama	ICT
Period 4	Drama	ICT
Period 5	PE	History
Period 6	Drama	ICT

* Student takes drama and PE over 1 year 6 periods per week

If you have read the section on Serlby Park, muttering every few minutes to yourself, 'It's ok for them', 'If only we could have their chances', 'Our schools are much too far apart', 'Our schools are much more urban', 'We have a bigger range of primary schools' or other such utterances, you are missing the point. I do not write of Serlby Park as the perfect solution. It was *our* solution, right for *our* situation, almost certainly wrong for *your* situation. The key is not the specifics of our solution but the method by which we found and then implemented it. The heartening thing for everyone should be that change is possible, and innovative solutions can be found locally. We were given 1,000 reasons why we should fail, but we found one very good reason for success: it was beneficial to the young people in our area!

If you still need persuading of the benefits of all-through education, these words are from Johnny Heather, Assistant Principal at Serlby Park, who also worked for five years in a 3–18 in Kenya.

Children thrive on responsibility, the feeling that they are worthwhile and are respected—this coupled with it being very 'uncool' to be antisocial while around children who are a lot younger. Add to this the fact that younger children feel it is part of their duty to report any signs of perceived wrongdoing and the fearsome spectre of rampant bullying doesn't happen. Peer group pressure regarding how children who are a lot younger are treated can be significant—not many teenagers would bat an eyelid if there were spats between a couple of their own or similar age groups but their responsible sides come to the fore if much younger children are the victims.

Without the bullying, what are we left with? Hero worship from younger to older pupils and caring from older to younger, linked with enthusiasm in abundance from younger pupils, experience and skills from older. These are the type of 'issues' we can all handle!

To me, experiences at school which enable pupils to gain more enjoyment, greater opportunities for developing responsibility and an ensuing increase in confidence levels are what we have often relegated due to pressures of league tables and endless examinations. I do not, however, feel that the pursuit of academic rigour and enjoyment, responsibility and confidence are mutually exclusive but should go hand in hand in any successful school and for any successful child's education.

Perhaps our final words should be from a description of a pupil's day from a few years in the future.

Callum's Day
October 2012

After breakfast in the school cafeteria, Callum retrieves his tablet from his locker and signs onto his learning space. He likes these moments in the morning when he can pick up messages from his teachers, with feedback on the assignments he submitted yesterday and comments on his progress within the online curriculum. This is monitored by an online mentor, who is fed the information about

Callum's progress on a unit by unit, subject by subject, basis. His mentor can also remotely access Callum's workspace at any time, with an instant onscreen messaging facility in use. The system also incorporates peer online discussion and he acts on the help he received yesterday from a Year 9 pupil who has responded to his plea for advice in algebra. He signs off.

Although only in Year 7 of this 3–18 all-through school, Callum has ICT/management information skills most adults would be proud of. The school is a registered 'thinking community' and independent approaches are the norm. He will leave with accreditation in subjects, as well as the 'softer skills' such as teamworking, interviewing, showing initiative—these are all accredited by the Chamber of Commerce so that local industry has a good measure of student aptitudes.

Callum can never understand why many of his peers in other schools have found the transition to Year 7 so difficult. The systems he has encountered are an extension of what he has known since he was 5. As well as the emphasis on interpersonal skills, Callum has been well immersed in the use of the 'Thinking Hats' and many other ways to develop independent thought processes. He has a Year 7 class teacher who he sees for two hours every day, working on cross-curricular projects—very much like his primary in fact. He also has specialist teachers obviously, but previously, in Years 4, 5 and 6, he had PE, French and Technology lessons with different teachers anyway. In fact, he still has the same rooms and teachers now. His friends, who have found the transition difficult, have never experienced an all-through school. Is this why they seem to have lost a little of the confidence he saw in them last year?

At 8.45am, Callum reports to his tutor, who is sitting with his laptop perusing Callum's records. He too has access to all academic progress data, as well as behavioural patterns and attendance. Callum's tutor discusses progress and then moves onto the new video-conferencing link Callum has set up for the class, joining with a dinosaur museum in Canada. He reassures his tutor that the video-conferencing room is booked and that the link will be ready when the tutor brings the class down. Since the new school was built with open learning, ICT-rich year areas, multimedia expertise has grown immensely. The old method of trying to book an ICT room greatly cut down the tutor's options. Now his class has full access to film-making, podcasting, video-conferencing and even a school radio station. Year 7 have a Monday and Tuesday slot on the radio, for which they must prepare a discussion. This time is also used in preparing their monthly citizenship assembly. IT is so much better than listening to the principal drone on. Year 7 now have a real stake in school issues and their voice is heard by the whole school.

A bigger advantage to the open learning areas is that Callum can now study subjects that the school may not even have teachers for. He wants to be a palaeontologist, with a specialism in geology. The local university is willing to offer a weekly lesson to Year 7. Some lessons are in school, in person, some are video-conferenced and some take place at the university. It has been a fantastic experience to sit in real lecture theatres and has made school study seem more worthwhile. One of his friends, who is an excellent mathematician, has been given special access to the university website so he can try the games they are building.

After the tutoring session, Callum returns to the open learning area for his Science session and logs back on. His Chemistry teacher is busy with a special tutorial with five students who have lost their way in the subject so Callum knows to click on his on-screen timetable. The lesson objective relates to chemical reactions, something the teacher has already introduced. Today's lesson comprises a video clip of 10 reactions, followed by an on-screen worksheet. Callum completes the task, which he finds easy and then sends it to the teacher's in-box. He goes out to the toilet and then comes back to his work space; a message is waiting. The teacher has given the five students a break and is concentrating on the work sent to him. Obviously, Callum underestimated the difficulty of the worksheet as a message reads, 'Thanks, but it needed 40 minutes, not 20! Numbers 6, 8 and 10 need more explanation, particularly in the reaction analysis section. If you don't understand number 10, watch the last five minutes of the podcast of yesterday's lesson-click on the lesson link below.'

Callum looks up. The teacher is now remotely accessing the screens of the whole calls, hurrying some along with help prompts. His teacher will bring the whole class back together tomorrow—it is usually a 50 ICT led/50 other classroom activity-led ratio, sometimes more, sometimes less, depending on the subject. When Callum mentions this to his friends at football, they can't believe it as they can only access ICT a few times a week. ICT-led lessons give the opportunity for teachers to spend more time with small groups of students. ICT is a lot cheaper than another teacher, so why don't some schools use them more? Callum's mum works as a nurse and a great proportion of NHS training is now online. It makes sense for schools to move much further in this direction.

Some of his classmates can't handle the extra freedom of ICT. Callum is one of the lucky 80 per cent who have this option. The other 20 per cent of students are taught in a much more structured, traditional way, as trust is an issue here—although as security software becomes more sophisticated, his ICT teacher thinks that this may change. Callum looks over into the classroom where 20 of his peers are sat listening to the teacher at the front of the class. Callum enjoys the introductory sessions and the plenaries structured in that same way, but he would go mad with boredom if it presented a majority stake in his learning.

The next session is a 'free-choice' option block. Trustworthy students are given the opportunity to choose something away from the core curriculum. Some are designing their own games, some are building their own websites. Many are creating lesson plans as they have been chosen to deliver lessons in their own specialisms to the lower years. Callum is using his expertise to teach a dinosaur unit to Year 4 and working with the technology, art and media departments to create an animated film. One of his other friends is taking basic Mandarin with the help of a work contact of his father in Shanghai and an interactive DVD. Callum's brother, in Year 10, already has four GCSE equivalents and an AS Level, taken from Year 9 onwards. Callum expects to better this as he will be taking two language GCSEs in Year 8 due to his five years' language experience through the primary years.

At lunchtime, the lockdown desks in the open learning area are used and half of the space becomes a recreational area for the students. The remainder remains work space for anyone who wants it over lunch. His dad tells him about the time when schools were built without any student recreational space and so wet lunchtimes put him in a really bad mood for the rest of the day. This applies to the exterior of the buildings as well. Callum now has specialist areas to take advantage of that mean he can be comfortable and get some fresh air as well. One of the areas is an outdoor dining area, where he can eat in pleasant, quieter surroundings. The food is good as well, cooked by his fellow students as part of their qualification in catering. The teaching rooms are situated to the side of the industrial kitchens and students have a vital say in what goes on the menu as they plan it themselves.

After lunch, Callum moves into his specialist blocks. The school has some amazing facilities and Callum never fails to be inspired by his surroundings. The art studio has fantastic natural light, with visiting artists providing the complementary inspiration. The performing arts studio has a real stage and theatre seating, with sprung flooring and soundproofed music rooms. The use of the facilities by the local community, particularly in putting on regular shows for residential homes in the area, means that relevance is always applied to his performance studies. In other areas as well, the science area, the technology rooms, the construction block, Callum has the opportunity to learn in quality surroundings. His brother has opted for graphics as a career path and works at a graphics company in the design department for three hours a week. All of the post-16 students have the opportunity for regular work placements, with work missed being posted on the learning platform as lesson podcasts. He has seen the podcasts and, whilst he would prefer to see the lesson in the flesh, he can understand the attraction of working in a proper workplace when he gets a little older. Plus he knows that he can pick up qualifications on an ongoing basis so, if targets look dicey he can always take a work break.

When he was asked to evaluate Year 7 experiences in an online survey last week, Callum did see both positives and negatives. On the positive side, he enjoys the freedom and choice of the curriculum, particularly the ICT possibilities which are endless. Some of the new games are directly linked to certain learning goals in many of his subjects and the way that he can interact with other students all around the world is so stimulating. He also enjoys accessing his ongoing targets and assessment tasks, receiving weekly updates from all his teachers, even when they are away. He has heard stories of hundreds of school hours wasted by using cover teachers as babysitters, but now ICT has given students a new direction so different from schools in the past. Teachers seem more enthusiastic too; they can now teach to smaller groups, focusing their lessons on areas of most need, rather than the 'middle ground'. They are more highly skilled than they have ever been because subject understanding is now underpinned by making cross-curricular reference to wider cross-curricular issues. Callum has been labelled as *Gifted and Talented* and this means that he is able to take his learning in any direction possible, often accessing the Year 9 curriculum.

On the negative side, he sometimes comes in some days without the energy to get things up and running by himself. This is alleviated somewhat by the more practically driven subjects such as Drama, Art, PE and suchlike but he still feels his self-discipline lacking at times. At least when the teacher talked at him in the past, he didn't have to think too much. Most of the time, work presented to him required the answering of some fairly easy exercises but at least he had pages of writing and he could show an end product. Now, when this apathy takes hold he visits the school learning coach who offers him the chance of focus or enrichment. His brother also tells him about the movement he used to enjoy between lessons as a chance to stretch his legs and kick some of his friends. Now, the fact that teachers move rooms, rather than students, has cramped this opportunity. Callum still needs to move to the specialist rooms but the corridors aren't the through ways they once were and the 'highs' of pushing and shoving described by his brother no longer exist.

The absence of bells, heads of year, smelly old toilets, archaic uniform rules and hard plastic chairs are all features of the past that he never knew but they did sound like fun. In many ways, the new learning community is more like a workplace; with lots of adults using facilities on site there isn't the same scope for mischief that his dad has described to him. Also, the site and all its facilities are open 16 hours a day so there isn't the same feeling that school is apart from the community. Callum certainly feels education is working for him, while his dad describes school as something that 'was done to him'. Boring, this lack of conflict really! His dad has described the spectacle of mob male mentality as class teachers and heads of year struggled with students who could never recognise the point in what they were doing and moreover, wanted the attention of the teacher and the class as if to prove an alternative superiority in lieu of academic prowess. With the bigger class sizes made possible with new technology and an open learning environment, more staff have now been released to work with smaller focus groups, concentrating on intervention strategies and alternative accreditation within the workplace and through vocational providers. More time with students seems to be the major requisite for improvements in behaviour and changing attitudes. There are still some good shouting matches with Year 10 and 11. Perhaps hormones would explain these!

His dad has some really scary stories about the times when everything depended on exam results at 16, 17 and 18. The main exam results at 16 and 18 only arrived after you'd left school! How was that supposed to motivate and inform you? Now each student is gaining accredited qualifications, sometimes in a written exam, sometimes not, when occasion and circumstance permit. Callum's dad called education in 2007 a one-stop shop, dominated by written exams. How that must have ruined the chances of so many kids. Very, very primitive!

When I first read Steve's suggestion for Callum's day I wondered if he was being idealistic, then I reconsidered. Did it make sense? Would it improve the current situation? Does the technology exist? Clearly the answer was 'Yes, yes, yes'. Some schools are actually well on the journey to Callum's Day whilst others aren't even out off the starting blocks—perhaps that is the problem. It is in our hands to decide if Callum's day is to remain a fairy tale, or to become the everyday story of twenty-first century education.

Conclusions or beginnings?

I started the book with a quote:

> *Do not follow where the path may lead.*
> *Go instead where there is no path and leave a trail.*

Harold R. McAlindon

I hope all these pages help you appreciate the importance of these words.

I hope you can:

a) understand why the old path should be avoided
b) appreciate why so many people have started new paths of their own
c) be inspired to begin a journey of your own.

I can promise you that the journey will not always be easy, in fact it is almost guaranteed to be uncomfortable for large sections! However, the road to improved transition brings so many benefits, it is worth every bead of perspiration.

So reach for your machete, and take that first step. If we all make our own start the pupils of the twenty-first century have a real chance of shaping our changing world.

Surely we owe them that?

You have the baton firmly in your hand; please make sure you pass it on safely!

Appendices

Appendix A

Questions for comparing primary and secondary experience

	Y6	Y7
% of day spent in classroom		
% of day spent moving between tasks		
% of day pupil smiles		
% of day taught as whole class		
% of lesson spent on active tasks		
% of lesson actively engaged in learning		
% of lesson where pupil engaged in assessment for learning (AFL)		
% of work in a lesson linked to other learning		
% of work differentiated for pupil		

Appendix B

Pupil questionnaire

Year: _____   **Male or Female:** _____

1. How much do you enjoy school?
    (Marks out of 10: 1 = I don't, 10 = brilliant)   [ ]

2. Would any of the teachers at school listen to you if you have a problem?
    (Please tick one box)

    ❑ Yes   ❑ No   ❑ Sometimes

3. If you have a problem who in school would you go to?

    _____

4. What's the best thing about school?

    _____

    _____

5. What's the worst thing about school?

    _____

    _____

6. Which ways help you most in your learning?

    _____

    _____

7. How do you think you learn best in school:

    ❑ My teacher telling me   [ ]
    ❑ Finding out for myself   [ ]   *Tick as many as you think are right for you*
    ❑ Working with a partner   [ ]
    ❑ Working with a big group   [ ]
    ❑ Working on the computer   [ ]
    ❑ Making things   [ ]   *Please show your no. 1 'best way' with a ***
    ❑ Acting things out   [ ]
    ❑ Showing others   [ ]

8. How often is learning fun? (*Please tick one box*)

    ❑ Always   ❑ Often   ❑ Occasionally   ❑ Never

9. My teachers try to do the best for me? (*Please tick one box*)

    ❑ Always   ❑ Most of the time   ❑ Sometimes   ❑ Never

10. How much of a day am I left to work on my own at school? (*Please tick one box*)

    ❑ Most of the day   ❑ ¾ of the day   ❑ ½ the day   ❑ ¼ day   ❑ None of the day

11. If you could improve your lessons in one way, what would it be?

_____

_____

_____

_____

12. If you could improve the whole school in one way, what would it be?

_____

_____

_____

_____

The following to be answered by primary pupils:

If you are a primary pupil, what worries you most about moving to the secondary phase?

_____

_____

_____

What excites you most about moving to secondary phase?

_____

_____

_____

The following to be answered by secondary pupils:

What do you enjoy most about the secondary phase?

_____

_____

_____

What did you prefer about the primary phase?

_____

_____

_____

Appendix C

Title	T shirt Business
Author	Natalie White
Year group	F ☐ 2 ☐ 3 ☐ 4 ☐ 5 ☒ 6 ☒ 7 ☒ 8 ☒ 9 ☒ 10 ☒ 11 ☐ 12 ☐ 13 ☐
Curriculum	
Time required	Min. 3 hours

Outline of activity

Pupils work in cross phase groups to set up and run a T shirt business. The T shirts are actually paper ones of the size frequently seen as stickers in car windows. The task is for the team to collaborate to decide on a design, buying ready made designs if required, and then developing a production line approach to producing quantities of the agreed design. Quality assurance is required by each team to avoid losing money/business.

Resources required

Rulers, scissors, coloured paper, calculators, squared paper

Instructions

Introduce task and aims

Give out budget and supplies—see www.droppingthebaton.com

Groups are given a 'pretend' start up loan of £200 to buy equipment (prices vary with demand). Pupils then buy a T shirt design on squared paper and must compete to make the most money. Sub standard T shirts will not be bought. Trade with other groups allowed. Groups may take out variable rate loans to expand.

Encourages group work across ages, risk taking, accounting, meeting deadlines.

Follow-up activity

Try it for real in school using computer/iron on transfer

Title	Drama Enterprise Anti bullying Event
Author	Catherine Hoyle and Louise Edwards
Year group	F ☐ 2 ☐ 3 ☐ 4 ☒ 5 ☒ 6 ☒ 7 ☐ 8 ☐ 9 ☐ 10 ☒ 11 ☐ 12 ☐ 13 ☐
Curriculum	Drama
Time required	Half day

Outline of activity

Y10 drama group prepare a role play depicting bullying/victims/the crowd. Presentation of a poem. Two Y10 pupils with six junior pupils working on various tasks to do with empathy, facial expression and feelings, ultimately to present a short play based on 'Bullying—see it, get help, stop it!'

Huge benefits in self belief development, for both young and older pupils.

Resources required

Sugar paper and pens

Large space

Instructions

Y10 perform first section of play showing a bully and a victim.

Bubble map in groups (two Y10s with six primary) with either bully in centre or victim in centre.

Choose four words and build up still images showing facial expressions and body language. Perform the images.

Two lines (one of bullies, one of victims). Bully says something, victim reacts. Choose examples to show.

Introduce poem adding in the crowd who stand by and say nothing—glad it's not them.

Group work—two lines and circle around (crowd/victim/bullies). Add in dialogue showing thoughts.

Y10s perform the whole play.

In groups produce a short play in three sections: 1) The bullying—see it, 2) Getting help, 3) Resulting in 'stop it'.

Perform for each other then in assembly.

Follow-up activity

Younger pupils write a piece of drama for the older ones to perform

Title	Court Case
Author	Lisa Tansley
Year group	F☐ 2☐ 3☐ 4☐ 5☐ 6☒ 7☐ 8☐ 9☒ 10☒ 11☐ 12☐ 13☐
Curriculum	
Time required	

Outline of activity

Students are given evidence/witness statements from fictitious court cases. Students take on roles of lawyers, clerks, ushers and witnesses—developing questions/preparing witnesses and putting on the trials.

Older pupils merely support the younger ones.

Learning to work independently and in teams. Developing oral confidence.

Resources required

Large space

Witness statements

Description of court and roles within it

Pens and paper

Instructions

Students given outline of magistrates court and procedures.

The case is outlined. Possible suggestions for suitable cases include:

> Biblical stories (such as The Good Samaritan)
> Historical issues (Trojan Horse—prosecuting the trespassers)
> Sociological issues (prosecuting a pickpocket)
> Cartoon stories (prosecuting Tom for attempted manslaughter of Jerry)
> School issues (the school bully—is there any defence?)

Split into teams (prosecution and defence) to prepare the case. Magistrate, usher, and clerk research their roles and law of case. Older pupils are just guides. Judge, magistrates, etc. are all younger pupils.

Perform (and record) the case in text and pictures.

Present the findings to pupils in primary and secondary.

Follow-up activity

All pupils write an account of the case from their viewpoint to be recorded on the website

Title	The School Bag
Author	Karen Elmy
Year group	F☐ 2☐ 3☐ 4☐ 5☐ 6☒ 7☒ 8☐ 9☐ 10☐ 11☐ 12☐ 13☐
Curriculum	
Time required	2 hours

Outline of activity

Pupils of Y6 work with Y7s who recently went through transition themselves. Using the focus of a school bag, items are considered in order of their merit and worries around the transfer can be aired in an unthreatening way.

This also helps Y6 pupils understand what may be required by the new school.

Resources required

School bag, containing a variety of appropriate items (e.g. planner, pens, pencils, ruler, rubber, change, etc.) and inappropriate items (Game Boy, make up, £20, etc.)

Instructions

Work in groups of six (three from each year group).

Each group opens a bag and decides which items are appropriate for school and which are not.

Encourage pupils to explain their answers in full.

Each group then produces their own poster explaining their decisions and why.

Each group then presents their findings to the group.

Improvements are suggested by the group and smaller posters/leaflets are designed and made.

The leaflets and posters are then distributed and displayed at each of the primary schools.

Versions should be displayed on the internet.

Follow-up activity

What will be in a school bag in 10 years' time?

Title	Improving a Shanty Town
Author	Ian Peach/Chris Robinson/David Coat
Year group	F☐ 2☐ 3☐ 4☐ 5☐ 6☒ 7☒ 8☒ 9☒ 10☒ 11☐ 12☐ 13☐
Curriculum	Geography
Time required	Half day

Outline of activity

Working in mixed age groups pupils develop their self confidence by considering a global issue together. By focusing on issues outside their own community pupils can strengthen the relationships within their own.

Groups look at the issues surrounding a shanty town—and consider what the priorities are and how things could be improved.

Develops group work, decision making , planning.

Resources required

Photocopied resources from *More Thinking Through Geography* by David Leat.

Video footage of favela in Brazil (or equivalent).

Photos in PowerPoint showing poor living conditions.

Instructions

Pupils in cross age groups of four to six.

Introduced to the concept of shanty towns and shown video and pictures demonstrating some of the issues raised by such settlements and the problems for people living there.

Resources are photocopied for each group—they must:

a) read and discuss each problem and decide what knock on effects they could have;

b) prioritise what needs dealing with under headings such as health, crime, safety, etc.;

c) plan how to spend money from the allocated cost sheet and allocate which schemes should be carried through;

d) plan a brief presentation to explain and justify decisions and spending.

Follow-up activity

Pupils become a delegation to visit the shanty town. What would they do and say?

Title	Group Art Project
Author	Ben Smith
Year group	F☐ 2☐ 3☐ 4☒ 5☐ 6☒ 7☒ 8☐ 9☐ 10☐ 11☐ 12☐ 13☐
Curriculum	Art
Time required	2–3 hours

Outline of activity

This is a project on image making where individuals construct smaller images which, when placed with others in the group, make a larger image.

This promotes group work and delivers the idea that working together can produce a bigger picture.

A variety of art movements can be used as the focus: Expressionism, Impressionism, Abstract Art, Dadaism, Surrealism, Pop Art, etc.

Resources required

Oil pastels, cards, images, handouts and props

Instructions

Introduce the pupils to the chosen art movement and at least one artist associated with that movement (e.g. Impressionism—Vincent Van Gogh) (see www.droppingthebaton.com for examples).

Using drama to illustrate the artist and their approach is useful at this point.

A picture of this artist will be chosen for the project. The picture will have a grid placed over it—the number of squares should equal the number of younger pupils. Each square will be given a code (e.g. A6).

Brief older pupils to be group leaders—each group leader will be given a unique section of the large picture.

Each will lead a group of younger pupils who will each produce a unique square in their own style coordinated by the older pupil. Each square to be labelled on the back with the name of the pupil and the square code.

The group will then assemble the picture on a large flat surface.

Follow-up activity

Older pupils take the mosaic picture to the primary phase and display it

Title	Orienteering
Author	Mrs Swindley
Year group	F☐ 2☐ 3☐ 4☐ 5☐ 6☒ 7☒ 8☐ 9☐ 10☐ 11☐ 12☐ 13☐
Curriculum	
Time required	2 hours

Outline of activity

An orienteering course is devised around the secondary school site.

Two Y6 pupils are paired with pupils from either Y7 or Y8 and then they attempt to complete the course in the shortest possible time.

Resources required

Compass for each pair, orienteering markers around school, cards and pencils

Instructions

An orienteering course is designed around the school. Eight markers each shown by a different letter from an eight letter word (e.g. ARMCHAIR) but the letters should not be used in the same order as in the word.

The start point will contain an instruction, distance and compass setting (e.g. 100m, 56°), then at each point the card will contain a letter and a further distance and setting.

Staff will be available at a central location from which clues can be bought (for a two minute time penalty) by the older pupil which will contain help such as 'Letter 6 is on the library wall'.

Pairs must return to a central point and their timing stops when they unmix the anagram.

Before commencing the activity all pupils will be shown a map of the school and introduced to their partner. Pairs will be introduced into the workings of a compass and the process by examples in the room. Pairs will be sent to the start point at two minute intervals.

There can be a second prize offered to the group who produce the best poster depicting their word.

Follow-up activity

Primary pupils could design a similar course around their own school for secondary visitors

Are You Dropping the Baton? © 2008 Crown House Publishing, David Harris

Title	Rockets
Author	Rick Huddart
Year group	F☐ 2☐ 3☐ 4☒ 5☒ 6☒ 7☒ 8☒ 9☒ 10☒ 11☒ 12☒ 13☐
Curriculum	Science
Time required	2 hours

Outline of activity

Cross phase groups of pupils work together to gain a better understanding of forces. This topic permeates the science curriculum and it is possible for pupils to access the task from different levels.

Whilst working on a common project the pupils develop a respect for each other's age group and the young pupils have secondary science, the secondary site and older pupils demystified.

Pupils will attempt to be the group to get the longest trajectory for a water rocket.

Resources required

Water rockets, pumps, ramps, trundle wheel, protractors

Instructions

Older pupils demo the water rocket.

Explain history of cannon balls and rockets (photos available at www.droppingthebaton.com).

Introduce ideas of angles/trajectory.

Divide into cross phase groups—older pupils to help with concepts and safety.

Plenary—prize giving for the best group, then extract the science learning.

Pupils produce posters showing their results.

Follow-up activity

Groups compete to produce the most aerodynamic nose cone

Title	Peer Learning
Author	Shirley Howe
Year group	F☐ 2☐ 3☐ 4☒ 5☒ 6☒ 7☐ 8☐ 9☐ 10☒ 11☐ 12☐ 13☐
Curriculum	Modern Foreign Languages (or any)
Time required	2 hours

Outline of activity

Older pupils are given ideas for a topic to teach and then, with the assistance of the teacher, they prepare the resources and lesson plan for a stand alone lesson in the chosen topic.

This develops self esteem and independence/teamworking skills amongst the older pupils along with raising their understanding of teaching and learning methods.

Younger pupils will raise their understanding of the new school and gain confidence in the maturity levels within the school.

Resources required

Laptop, MP3, laminator and pouches, photocopies, pens, Blu Tac

Instructions

Modern Foreign Languages (MFL) would make an excellent topic for this focus, but any subject would be suitable as long as the material delivered is suitable for a primary curriculum.

If MFL is chosen as the focus then a small vocabulary topic (such as food) should be identified. Y10 pupils are introduced to the concept of lesson planning and reminded of learning styles and the need to deliver to the variety within a group.

Each group of Y10s are given a sub topic and asked to develop a lesson plan. The teacher will help shape the pupils' plans.

The secondary pupils then visit the primary school (or deliver at the secondary site on a transition event).

The Y10s deliver 20 minute sessions to the primary pupils.

At the end of the session there should be time for a question and answer session about life at the secondary school.

Follow-up activity

Groups of primary pupils prepare a lesson about the local community for secondary pupils

Title	Outdoor Adventure Activities (1)
Author	Lucy Simister
Year group	F☐ 2☐ 3☐ 4☐ 5☒ 6☒ 7☒ 8☐ 9☐ 10☐ 11☐ 12☐ 13☐
Curriculum	PE/Outdoor Education
Time required	45 minutes

Outline of activity

Pupils are placed in mixed age groups—two from each group (total of six in team). They have to work as a group to solve a practical (exploding bomb) task. Once they have developed a strategy they have to complete the practical activity in the shortest time possible. Three attempts are allowed for each team.

This activity postiviely promotes team work and helps to develop trust between pupils of the different age groups.

Resources required

Four exploding buckets (plastic bucket with six 3m ropes from each, evenly spaced and coming out from the rim like rays from a central sun—each bucket has a false cardboard bottom 5cm from the rim and six tennis balls on this base).

Instructions

The buckets should be set up as described above (to see photographs of the bomb visit www.droppingthebaton.com).

Pupils are put into mixed age teams of six.

The task is explained. The delicate exploding bomb is represented by the bucket containing six explosive grenades (tennis balls). If any of these fall out of the bucket there will be a terrible explosion and the run will have to restart.

There is a 50m course laid out—the task is to move the bucket from one end to the other without it (or any of the balls) touching the ground.

The teams cannot touch the bucket with anything and can only pick it up by pulling on the end of the long rope—clearly another team member must provide an opposing force with the opposite rope! All six team members spread themselves around the bucket and together raise the bucket without spilling any grenades! If any balls fall the team must go back to the start—the clock carries on running.

The best of three times is recorded—the fastest time overall is the winning team.

Follow-up activity

See other activities or team could be given A4 paper to design (and wear) team logo/flag

Title	Outdoor Adventure Activities (2)
Author	Lucy Simister
Year group	F☐ 2☐ 3☐ 4☐ 5☒ 6☒ 7☒ 8☐ 9☐ 10☐ 11☐ 12☐ 13☐
Curriculum	PE/Outdoor activities
Time required	30 mins

Outline of activity

Teams of six mixed age pupils (two each from Y5, Y6 and Y7) are set up.

Each team has to get across a shark infested river on six small stepping stones.

This is modelled by representing the river banks as two lines and only allowing travel between when standing on an object.

The team to do so the quickest wins.

This activity promotes team work and mutual trust as well as problem solving.

Resources required

Four sets of five 'stepping stones'—these can be small tyres, cardboard pieces (A3 size), small mats or towels (bar towel size), two river banks at least 5m apart

Instructions

Pupils are placed into mixed age teams of six (two from each age group).

The scenario is set—the team must all get to the other side of the dangerous river using only the stepping stones. They must all travel over together and cannot move a stepping stone whilst they are standing on it. The team to make the trip in the shortest time wins. Anyone putting a foot (or hand) in the 'water' results in their team going back and starting again.

Teams start (and move) in a vertical line (snake) across the river.

Teams are given five minutes to discuss their tactics before beginning.

Most teams develop a strategy which involves the last two in the line sharing a stepping stone (i.e. whole team holds onto each other), whilst the last one picks up the final stepping stone, passes it forward along the line to the front person who puts it a small step in front of themselves, and then the whole line moves forward and repeats the process.

If teams find it too difficult to avoid falling into the water, time penalties can be added for each step rather than restarting the crossing after each mistake.

The best of two crossing times is used to select the winner.

Follow-up activity

See other activities or team could be given A4 paper to design (and wear) team logo/flag

Title	Outdoor Adventure Activities (3)
Author	Lucy Simister
Year group	F☐ 2☐ 3☐ 4☐ 5☒ 6☒ 7☒ 8☐ 9☐ 10☐ 11☐ 12☐ 13☐
Curriculum	PE/Outdoor Activities
Time required	30 mins

Outline of activity

Two teams of (12–16) mixed age pupils are set up. There should be an even split of age groups.

The pupils then have to carry out a 'walking the plank' activity where they have to use team work to arrange themselves into various orders.

This activity is fun, builds mutual trust and team building and also helps pupils familiarise themselves with names.

Resources required

Two benches (more for larger numbers), and mats to run alongside both sides of each bench in case of falls.

Instructions

Pupils are split into two teams of equal numbers and age profile.

Each team is asked to stand in a line alongside one of the two benches which are parallel to each other about 3m apart.

Each team should then be told to arrange their line so that they are not standing next to anyone else of their own age group (a teacher help may be needed to start this off).

Pupils should then be asked to introduce themselves to the person either side of them.

The scenario is now set—the team must all stand up on the bench in their current order—all facing the teacher at one end of the benches.

The surrounding floor has been electrocuted/filled with sharks, etc.

Each team must now arrange themselves in alphabetical order by first name—they must pass each other on the bench and must not touch the floor (or nearby walls, etc.). They can support each other. Any touching of the floor etc. will result in a 30 second time penalty for each error.

Once completed, follow up activities could include: arrange in alphabetical order by surname, arrange by date in the year of their birthday, etc.

Follow-up activity

See other activities or team could be given A4 paper to design (and wear) team logo/flag

Title	Card Making
Author	Carol Wood
Year group	F ☐ 2 ☐ 3 ☐ 4 ☒ 5 ☒ 6 ☒ 7 ☒ 8 ☒ 9 ☒ 10 ☒ 11 ☐ 12 ☐ 13 ☐
Curriculum	Art/Craft
Time required	2 hours

Outline of activity

In mixed age groups pupils design and produce greetings cards for the next relevant season/ birthday.

The aim is to produce as many identical cards as possible, where each member of the team has done something on every card.

This is a 'production line' activity, but enables everyone to be involved and to work to their strengths. It is an excellent way to build team work and trust.

Resources required

Card of a variety of shapes, colours and textures, reprinted letters/ transfers, stamps and ink, crêpe paper, shiny paper/foil, glitter, glue, beads, etc.

Instructions

Pupils are put into mixed age group teams. One pupil (who has been briefed and prepared for the activity) is asked to be company leader.

Each team is to become a card making company. Their first task is to decide on a company name and logo. They will then be given a theme for their card making (Christmas/Easter/ Valentine's Day/ Mother's Day/birthday, etc.).

Each team must together design a card. They must produce 12 identical cards and each member of their team must do something on each card. The leader of each team will get ideas from the team in a 20 minute design session (during this time no large scale making is allowed). At the end of the time the teacher is shown the rough design (and can/should make constructive suggestions).

Teams then have a 10 minute planning session to allocate tasks—remembering that everyone must contribute to every card.

The teams then have one hour for the production line, during which time they must aim to make 12 identical cards. They should undergo their own quality control and may choose their best 12 cards.

Winners are chosen on quality, similarity and full group involvement.

Follow-up activity

Team could produce posters and sell them for charity

Title	Uni Hockey
Author	Johnny Heather
Year group	F ☐ 2 ☐ 3 ☐ 4 ☐ 5 ☒ 6 ☒ 7 ☒ 8 ☒ 9 ☐ 10 ☐ 11 ☒ 12 ☒ 13 ☒
Curriculum	Sport
Time required	1 hour

Outline of activity

Uni Hockey is a sport which enables all ages and abilities to gain success, promoting enthusiasm and fitness as well as developing team skills.

Older pupils (Y11–12) can act as team coaches and referees.

By creating a mixed age team, pupils gain confidence and younger pupils are less daunted by transition issues.

Resources required

Indoor gym or sports hall, Uni Hockey sticks, puck, whistle and scoreboard (whiteboard).

Instructions

Divide pupils into mixed age group teams—if using pupils in Y5, Y6 and Y7 then three from each age group form a team. Each team is attached to a coach, who is one of the older (Y11/12) pupils.

Coaches ensure pupils know each other's names and undergo 30 minutes of skills training (control of puck, passing, etc.).

All pupils are reminded of the rules of the game (for a summary of rules see www.droppingthebaton.com).

Each team can be designing and drawing their team flag while they are waiting for their turn.

Either play a championship/league system, or if there are three teams 'winner stays on' is successful.

Coaches support and advise their teams during play, and have practice sessions while waiting.

Follow-up activity

All pupils produce poetry, drawings, stories related to Uni Hockey for a display

Title	Chess Championship
Author	Phil Palmer
Year group	F ☐ 2 ☐ 3 ☐ 4 ☐ 5 ☒ 6 ☒ 7 ☒ 8 ☒ 9 ☐ 10 ☐ 11 ☐ 12 ☐ 13 ☐
Curriculum	General
Time required	2 hours/after school sessions

Outline of activity

Inter year group chess championship.

A speed version of chess is best used for this activity.

Pupils initially play matches against pupils from a different year group.

A chess ladder encourages players to meet and play a variety of pupils.

Chess is an excellent non threatening way of developing relationships and gives self esteem to a variety of pupils.

Resources required

12 chess sets, tables, chairs, stop watches/clocks, squash ladder type of board (see www.droppingthebaton.com for examples)

Instructions

Initially hold a meeting at both primary and secondary phases asking for pupils interested in joining a chess club to come along. At the meeting explain the rules for 10 minute chess (see www.droppingthebaton.com) in which at 10 minutes the pupil with the highest score of captured pieces is declared the winner.

Ask pupils to complete a simple chess club card (see www.droppingthebaton.com), outlining interests, hobbies and school likes/dislikes. Also ask them to grade their chess ability as Never Played, Beginner, Average, Good or Grand Master.

Arrange a joint meeting where starter pupils are paired together with a more experienced player as a coach/referee. At this meeting explain the rules of the chess ladder and show the beginning ladder (this should be in a fairly random order, but with beginners towards the bottom (or on a different ladder).

The league should be constructed with no player next to one from the same year group.

Matches are played between any two players adjacent in the league. If the lower player wins the places swap positions.

Follow-up activity

A chess display is made by the pupils in each school

Title	Weaving a Fence
Author	Joy Sweeney
Year group	F ☒ 2 ☒ 3 ☒ 4 ☒ 5 ☒ 6 ☒ 7 ☒ 8 ☒ 9 ☒ 10 ☒ 11 ☒ 12 ☒ 13 ☒
Curriculum	
Time required	2–3 hours

Outline of activity

Pupils of all ages are gathered together under the common theme of spring.

A piece of 3D art is to be produced from contributions of every age.

Pupils weave items relating to spring and the school into the 'fence' which is sited at one of the schools.

Prior to the event older pupils are briefed to produce designs as a kick start for the process.

This activity promotes trust between different age groups and provides a constant reminder of work between the phases.

Resources required

A 'blank' fence and a variety of natural and manmade materials (e.g. ribbon, grass, leaves, paper, fabric, raffia, plastic, etc.)

Instructions

A planning group of mixed age pupils meet with the art teacher to identify a suitable length of fence (at either primary or secondary phase). This can be a mesh or strut fence but should be free of obstructions. The group should undertake its cleaning in advance of the activity day!

The meeting should discus an outline design for the fence (e.g. a theme such as spring, new beginnings, growth, Easter, change).

Once a theme is decided the possible materials are viewed and then, back in the age groups, a variety of designs are produced.

The process continues with an hour long design session—all designs are considered and a decision is made about the final design. The art teacher then helps turn the design into an action plan, i.e. what materials to use and how to fix them.

On a suitable day mixed age groups of pupils are given specific tasks and the fence is woven together. The process should be regularly stopped for a review—stepping back and amending the plan.

Digital photographs should be taken during the process and of the finished product.

Follow-up activity

Use the digital photographs to produce displays in each school

Title	Juggling
Author	Steve Geraghty
Year group	F ☐ 2 ☐ 3 ☐ 4 ☐ 5 ☒ 6 ☒ 7 ☒ 8 ☒ 9 ☐ 10 ☒ 11 ☐ 12 ☐ 13 ☐
Curriculum	
Time required	Half day

Outline of activity

Pupils of different ages learn a new skill together.

Juggling develops the connection between right and left brain and is an excellent activity in its own right.

Pupils of different ages are encouraged to develop relationships and to support each other by helping each other to develop individual skills, but also practising paired and group juggling.

Resources required

Balls for juggling

Uncluttered space

Instructions

Introduction

One ball individual

One ball paired

Two balls paired

Two balls individual

Three balls paired

Three balls individual

Pupils then make a video showing how to learn to juggle. These pupils then teach other pupils at both primary and secondary levels.

A demonstration of juggling skills could be made at assemblies of each participating school.

Follow-up activity

Upload a jpeg of the activities onto the web

Title	Treasure Hunt
Author	Lia Smith
Year group	F☐ 2☐ 3☐ 4☒ 5☒ 6☒ 7☒ 8☒ 9☒ 10☐ 11☐ 12☐ 13☐
Curriculum	Library/Literacy
Time required	1 hour + 2 hours planning

Outline of activity

Pupils from different age groups work together in teams to discover clues hidden in books in the library.

They improve their knowledge of the library and by working across ages gain a wider insight into a broader variety of books as well as developing team working skills.

The questions can either be set in advance for teams to compete against each other, or if more time is available the teams can prepare questions for each other.

Resources required

Clues (examples www.droppingthebaton.com), paper, name badges if teams are unfamiliar with each other

Instructions

Ensure pupils of different age groups are mixed.

Teacher to facilitate introducing pupils to each other. Encourage older pupils to ensure all are involved, but insist that the team captain is one of the younger pupils.

Introduce all pupils to the library and ensure someone in each team is fully aware of how to use the reference system being used.

Walk through an example clue, demonstrating how the team discuss and plan their strategy.

Follow-up activity

Ask pupils to plan a library treasure hunt for teaching staff!

Title	Charity Event
Author	Joy Sweeney
Year group	F☐ 2☐ 3☒ 4☒ 5☐ 6☐ 7☐ 8☐ 9☐ 10☐ 11☒ 12☒ 13☒
Curriculum	
Time required	Half day + extra sessions

Outline of activity

Pupils of different ages choose a charity to focus their work on.

The groups then plan joint ways of raising money and carry out their plans at all ages.

This is a good way of building up trust between phases as well as developing a social conscience.

Focusing the relationship on external factors rather than on the transition itself can lower the fear of transition.

Resources required

Posters and information about a variety of charity events (Children in Need and Comic Relief produce information packs to support fundraising).

Instructions

Separate school councils or interested groups of pupils nominate charities to be the focus of the event.

Nominations are then considered at a special mixed age group meeting when a decision on the focus charity is made. The group then decides on ideas to raise money for this—these should all involve some degree of cross-phase working. Ideas could include: older pupils dressing up as characters for photographs with the younger ones, charity concert, making items for sale within the school, producing a calendar containing art work from each phase, producing a transition magazine.

Once a favoured approach is decided pupils should then allocate tasks such as poster production.

All the mixed age group must be involved in summarising the work and presenting the money to the charity.

Follow-up activity

Produce a newspaper article recording the event and send to all parents

Title	Sky High and Beyond
Author	Tricia Brownsed
Year group	F☐ 2☐ 3☐ 4☐ 5☐ 6☒ 7☒ 8☐ 9☐ 10☐ 11☐12☐ 13☐
Curriculum	Science
Time required	5–6 weeks

Outline of activity

A team challenge involving all pupils split into different groups of four. Two Y7 students will work with two Y6 pupils. The cross-phase, science-based enterprise challenge would ideally be set using an e-learning platform after the Teacher Briefing ahead of the event. Teams will have to use the e-learning platform to communicate their ideas and must show evidence that everyone in the team has contributed.

The follow up activity will build on additional knowledge and understanding gained on the day at the secondary.

The final outcomes will be submitted and assessed after National Science Week. The best outcomes will go on the school website for anyone to vote online.

Resources required

Instructions

Films like *Super Size Me* and documentaries like Al Gore's *An Inconvenient Truth*, all attempt to alert us to the fact that our bodies and planet are balanced living things.

Eight Y7 students from three secondary schools and eight Y6 from their partner schools will form 'companies' who will then work as teams to take up various enterprise challenges relating to science and arising from farm activities and produce.

The five to six week 'event' comprises a programme of investigations leading to a day of workshops, which will be delivered by educationalists, specialist enthusiasts and professionals from the organic farming industry, and a team challenge involving all pupils split into different groups of four.

Two Y7 students will work with two Y6 pupils to accept the science-based enterprise

Follow-up activity

Displays made in all schools and assemblies

Useful organisations

The Innovation Unit
28–30 Grosvenor Gardens
London SW1W 0TT

ITL
Box 60
9 Perseverance Works
Kingsland Road
London E2 8DD
Tel: 0709 239 9617
email: admin@independentthinking.co.uk
website: www.independentthinking.co.uk

SSAT
16th Floor West, Milbank Tower
21-24 Millbank
London SW1P 4QP

Serlby Park (a 3–18 Business & Enterprise Learning Community)
Whitehouse Road
Bircotes
Doncaster DN11 8EF
Tel 01430 82726
e-mail: office@serlbypark.notts.sch.uk

Sue Clarke
Innovations Officer
Devon County Council
County Hall
Topsham Road
Exeter
Devon EX2 4Q
email: sue.clarke@devon.gov.uk

CATS (Consortium of All Through Schooling)
Office:
The Glebe
Ipsley Lane
Ipsley
Redditch B98 0AP
Tel: 01527 529461 Fax: 01527 500341
email: info@allthroughdchooling.org
website: www.allthroughschooling.org

Bibliography

Abbott, J. & Ryan, T. (2000) *The Unfinished Revolution: Learning, human behaviour, community and political paradox*. Network Education Press, Stafford.

Christensen, L., Karp, S. (2003) *Rethinking School Reform*. Milwaukee, WI: Rethinking Schools Ltd.

Dryden, G. & Vos, J. (2005) *The Learning Revolution*, Network Education Press, Stafford.

Educational Survey of Tattnall County, Georgia (Atlanta: Department of Education, 1916).

Georgia Department of Education Annual Report, 1895.

Gilbert, I. (2002) *Essential Motivation in the Classroom*, Routledge, Abingdon.

Gilbert, I. (2005) *Little Owl's Book of Thinking*, Crown House Publishing, Carmarthen.

Gilbert, I., et al. (2006) *The Big Book of Independent Thinking*, Crown House Publishing, Carmarthen.

Goodlad, J., Bromley, C. & Goodlad, S. (2004) *Education for everyone: Agenda for education in a democracy*. San Francisco, CA: Jossey-Bass.

Goodlad, John I. (2004) *Romances with Schools: A life of education*. New York: McGraw-Hill.

Hadley, J. (2001) *African-American Life on the Southern Hunting Plantation*. Chicago, IL: Arcadia Publishing.

Handy, C. B. (1994) *The Empty Raincoat*. London: Hutchinson.

Hargreaves, D. H. (2007) *System Redesign-1: The road to transformation in education*. Specialist Schools and Academies

Hayhoe, R. (1984) *Contemporary Chinese education*. London: Croom Helm.

Holdsworth, J. C. & Deng, M. (2005) *From Unconscious to Conscious Inclusion: Meeting Special Education Needs in West China*. Paper presented at Inclusive and Supportive Education Conference in Glasgow, United Kingdom.

Jacobson, S., Emihovich, C., Helfrich, J., Petrie, H. & Sevenson, B. (1998) *Transforming schools and schools of education: A new vision for preparing educators*. Thousand Oaks, CA: Corwin Press.

Johnson, B. & Christensen, L. (2004) *Educational research: Quantitative, qualitative and mixed approaches (2nd ed.)*. Boston, MA: Allyn and Bacon.

Joiner, Oscar H., ed. (1979) *A History of Public Education in Georgia*. Columbia, SC: R. L. Bryan Company.

One-Room School in Greenfield Village: Teacher's Guide (2007) Dearborn, MI.

One-Room School Links (2007), Northern Illinois University. www.cedu.niu.edu/blackwell/linkschool.htm

Orr, D. A. (1950) *History of Education in Georgia*. Chapel Hill, NC: University of North Carolina Press.

Piaget, J. (2001) *The language and thought of the child.* Routledge Classics.

Prashnig, B. (2004) *The Power of Diversity*, Network Education Press, Stafford.

Sanders, W. (2001) *The Sanders model: Tennessee value-added Assessment System.* Presentation to the GA EPAAC, Annual fall retreat. Macon GA.

Sanders, W. & Rivers, J. (1996) *Cumulative and residual effects of teachers on future student academic achievement.* Research Progress Report. Knoxville: University of Tennessee Value-Added Research and Assessment Center.

Shoerner, G., ed. (2000) *Under One Roof.* Country School Association of America. http://csaa.typepad.com/country_school_assocatio/2006/09/index.html

Stringfield, S., Ross, S. & Smith, L. (1996) *Bold plans, for school restructuring.* Mahwah, NJ: Lawrence Erlbaum Associates.

Wheatley, M. J. (1999) *Leadership and the New Science: Discovering order in a chaotic world.* Berrett-Koehler Publishers, San Francisco.

Wright., S., Horn, S. & Sanders, W. (1997) Teacher and classroom context effects on student achievement: Implications for teacher evaluation. *Journal of Personnel Evaluation in Education*, 111(57), pp. 57–67.

Index

ISBN: 978-190442438-3

Independent Thinking Ltd is a unique network of educational innovators and practitioners who work throughout the UK and abroad with children and their teachers and school leaders. It was established in 1993 by Ian Gilbert to 'enrich young people's lives by changing the way they think – and so to change the world' by delivering in-school training, development, coaching and consultancy. Ian achieved his objective by gathering together a disparate group of associates – specialists in the workings of the brain, discipline, emotional intelligence, ICT, motivation, using music in learning, creativity and dealing with the disaffected. This book is a collection of the best work from his associates, including:

- 'How the 'Brian' Works' by Andrew Curran, Consultant Paediatric Neurologist at Alder Hey Children's Hospital

- 'Living a Creative Life' by Roy Leighton, author, coach, trainer and lecturer at the European Business School

- 'Build the Emotionally Intelligent School' by Michael Brearley, author, trainer, coach and former head teacher

- 'On Love, Laughter and Learning' by David Keeling, actor, drummer, magician, comedian and educationalist

- 'Music and the Mind' by Nina Jackson, opera-trained music teacher and a specialist in special needs, music therapy and teacher training

- 'The Disciplined Approach' by Jim Roberson, former American football player, coach and teacher

- 'Peek! Copy! Do! The Creative Use of IT in the Classroom' by Guy Shearer, Director of the Learning Discovery Centre, Northampton

- 'The Best is the Enemy of the Good' by Matt Gray, theatre director and teacher at Carnegie Mellon University

The motto of Independent Thinking Ltd is to 'do things no one does or do things everyone does in a way no one does'. With a chapter from each of the associates plus an introduction and commentary by Ian Gilbert, this book is meant to be dipped into and to get you thinking for yourself – thinking about what you do, why you do what you do and whether doing it that way is the best thing at all.

www.crownhouse.co.uk

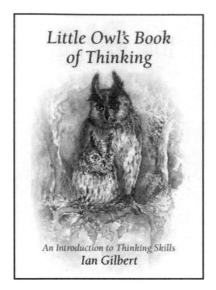

**Little Owl's Book
of Thinking**

An Introduction to Thinking Skills
Ian Gilbert

ISBN: 978-190442435-2

*"How do you do it, Dad?" asked Benny, the owlet. (For those of you who don't
know, an owlet is a little owl, like a piglet is a little pig, and outlet is a little out but not
all the way.)*

*"Do what?" said Big Owl, Benny the Owlet's Dad, who being grown up didn't
need letters after his name.*

"Be so wise and all knowing?"

*"Well," replied the wise, middle-aged owl, "I think it's just an owl thing. To be honest
I am not really sure how I got to be omniscient."*

*"Will I be wise like you when I'm all grown-up?" asked Benny, who was too small
to appreciate semantic irony.*

"Well," said Big Owl, "that depends on how you think."

"Think about what?" asked Benny.

"No. Just think," came the reply.

This brilliant little book continues in this entertaining style to describe the seven lessons
Benny receives from his wise old father, keen to teach his son how to think and think well.
Ideal for teachers, parents and older children, this book is an excellent method of introducing
the concept of thinking skills and why they are so important.

"Extremely accessible to anyone's first introdution to thinking skills. Well presented in a
non-threatening manner."
Joanne Strachan, School of Life Long Learning, Sunderland University

"... amusing, witty, thought provoking and an original way of introducing thinking skills."
Dr David George, Educational Consultant, Gifted Education

"... another gem from the pen of Ian Gilbert! From the opening lines the reader is taken on an
exploration – of how, what, why and where we think and learn but also an exploration of
oneself, one's relationship with people, places and the mysteries of the natural and created
world."
**Kathy Alcock, Principal Lecturer in Education,
Canterbury Christ Church University College**

www.crownhouse.co.uk

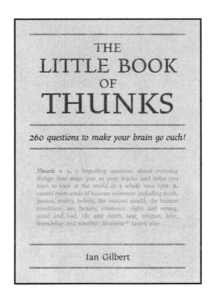

THE
LITTLE BOOK
OF
THUNKS

260 questions to make your brain go ouch!

Thunk n. 1. a beguiling question about everyday things that stops you in your tracks and helps you start to look at the world in a whole new light. 2. covers most areas of human existence including truth, justice, reality, beliefs, the natural world, the human condition, art, beauty, existence, right and wrong, good and bad, life and death, war, religion, love, friendship and whether Marmite™ tastes nice.

Ian Gilbert

ISBN: 978-184590062-5

260 questions to make your brain go ouch!

If I borrow a million pounds am I a millionaire?

Could a fly cause an aeroplane to crash?

Are you man-made or natural?

Do dogs believe in God?

When you comb your hair is it art?

A Thunk is a beguiling question about everyday things that stops you in your tracks and helps you start to look at the world in a whole new light.

The author guides you through the origins and uses of Thunks and demonstrates how this powerful little book can develop philosophical thinking for all ages … remember there are no right or wrong answers to these questions. How liberating is that …?

"… a delightful book written by an inspired thinker."
Alistair Smith, best-selling author and leading trainer

"… rich with ideas on how to implement Philosophy in your school."
Lyn Walsh, Gifted and Talented Strand Coordinator

"A Thunk can be used to warm up students of all ages; to entertain children on a car journey; or round off an evening with friends!"
Mike Cousins, Northamptonshire Raising Standards Partnership Trust

"… the most flabby brain muscles in the room (including mine) have been encouraged to flex and tone confidently without fear of revealing the 'wrong' mental Lycra."
Jeanne Fairs, Media Studies/English Teacher

"… an instantaneous passport to the very best of children's thinking."
Phil Beadle, Education Guardian columnist, award winning teacher and author of *Could do Better*

www.crownhouse.co.uk

ISBN: 978-190442481-9

The Buzz is an exciting collection of interactive techniques blending the richness and energy of NLP and personality type theory to inform and motivate young people to make positive life choices.

… a dedicated website www.thebuzzbook.co.uk features:

- free MP3 downloads as well as …
- 'Ask the Buzz' an online advice service for teens

"This is by far, the best motivational resource I have come across for young people and for the practitioners who work with young people."

"It puts young people in control of their own behaviour, relationships and emotions and is a truly excellent aid to decision making and self development."

Michaela Gill, Training Officer, Trafford Connexions and Youth Service

"Excellent. … a relentlessly positive message but never patronising that should do much to help raise self esteem and confidence in the reader. … helpful techniques, tips and tricks for all."

Matt Deakin, Careers Advisory Service, Durham University

"A particularly useful tool in helping young people to understand themselves and their world and in helping young people who are experiencing difficulties to think they can do something positive to change their lives. … a great resource."

Mike Soanes, Barnardo's

"… accessible, engaging and entertaining."

Stewart Farrar, Assistant Regional Manager, VT Careers Management West Sussex

David Hodgson is a Master Practitioner and Trainer of NLP, has the British Psychological Society Level A&B, a Diploma in Careers Guidance and a Diploma in Management. He is a Training Consultant in the North East working with young people and those who work with them on motivation, goal setting, life skills and employability.

ISBN: 978-184590070-0

The Learner's Toolkit is an essential resource for supporting the SEAL framework in secondary schools and for all those teaching 11-16 year olds. It contains everything you need to create truly independent learners, confident and resilient in their ability to learn and learn well. The book contains 52 lessons to teach 52 competencies. Each has teacher's notes on leading the lesson and a CD-ROM in the back of the book has all the student forms and worksheets necessary for the lessons. Lessons include:

- getting to know yourself
- persistence and resilience
- controlling moods
- building brain power
- developing willpower
- prioritising and planning

- taking responsibility for your own life
- setting goals for life
- caring for your mind and body
- asking questions
- pushing yourself out of your comfort zone

Possessing these vital competencies will help students learn better and be able to contribute more effectively in school. It will also enable them to thrive in the increasingly fast-paced world of the 21st Century.

"This book supports the new Secondary Curriculum in its efforts to promote Personal Development and links diversity to the Social Emotional Aspects of Learning (SEAL) Framework for secondary schools. It gives teachers starting points, plans and examples to help them use their own ideas to support the progress of young people in the most vital of all areas of learning ... how to cope with and contribute to the world in which they find themselves.î"

Mick Waters, Director of Curriculum, QCA

Jackie Beere is a consultant trainer and School Improvement partner, having been headteacher at Campion School, Northants. She spent three years as an Advanced Skills Teacher leading and implementing innovative Teaching and Learning initiatives including KS3 and 4 Learning to Learn and Thinking Skills programmes. In November 2002 Jackie was awarded the OBE for her services to education.

THE LITTLE BOOK
OF BIG STUFF
ABOUT THE BRAIN

The true story of your amazing brain

THIS BOOK
IS ABOUT
YOUR BRAIN!

Andrew Curran
Edited by Ian Gilbert

ISBN: 978-184590085-4

Dr Andrew Curran is a practising paediatric neurologist in Liverpool who is also committed to using his extraordinary knowledge of the workings of the human brain to make a difference in the educational experience of all young people. He's involved with Manchester University's Department of Education in developing research ideas looking at the use of emotional literacy in our classrooms.

Designed as a cover to cover read which leaves the reader with a working knowledge of the human brain from its first evolution 2 billion years ago to the present day. It is a light-hearted look at the brain aimed at a lay audience. It especially focuses on the neurobiology of emotional intelligence and in many ways is the neurobiological explanation of why emotional intelligence is so important to health, wealth and happiness.

The Little Book of Big Stuff About the Brain is about understanding why emotional health is so important. It is a book about structure and function – and the immensely reassuring fact that there is nothing occult or sinister or hidden about our emotional selves – there is just a whole pile of circuitry that can be adjusted and changed and remodelled. Emotional damage is repairable, painful memories can be unlearned, and debilitating conditions such as post traumatic stress disorder can be placed firmly in the past. There is nothing about ourselves that we can't fundamentally change if we are prepared to do the work required. This means that no matter how deep the damage runs, there is still hope that it can (eventually) be unlearned.

The most important message in this book – emotions and our emotional brains - underpin most of what we are and how we express ourselves from how we brush our hair to how we solve complex social and intellectual questions.

www.crownhouse.co.uk

ISBN: 978-189983665-9

This teaching resource aptly demonstrates how pupils can approach their work, and their future, with confidence, ambition, optimism and integrity. Providing practical strategies for integrating Emotional Intelligence across the curriculum, Emotional Intelligence in the Classroom reveals the power of emotion in learning. It explains the fundamentals of Emotional Intelligence (EI) and Emotional Quotient (EQ) and presents original research on the impact of EI on learning

A thoroughly practical work, containing numerous reproducible resources for the classroom teacher.

"Michael Brearley has provided a succinct and readable summary of what Emotional Intelligence can offer to the learning repertoire of children. In a clear and accessible style the book draws on the theory of emotional and multiple intelligence and pins this down into a series of structured activities for classrooms. This book is a must for those who are serious about a multi-layered approach to learning."

Alistair Smith, Author and leading educational trainer

"*Emotional Intelligence in the Classroom* by Michael Brearley provides a clear account of some practical strategies for integrating emotional intelligence across the school curriculum."

Professor Katherine Ware, Health Education

Former headmaster Michael Brearley is widely experienced in secondary education, and has a long-standing interest in engaging students more fully in their learning. Brearley's applied research at the University of East Anglia (UK) focused on teacher behaviour and how it impacted on students' learning; a later study examined the role of mediation and the work of Carl Rogers. His recent research into Emotional Intelligence has explored its practical application in the business and educational sectors, particularly its effect upon performance as a teacher and leader.

www.crownhouse.co.uk

Independent Thinking Ltd was set up in 1993 to 'Enrich children's lives by changing the way they think - and so to change the world'. Since that time this unique organisation, led by its founder Ian Gilbert, has worked across the UK and around the world with young people, teachers, school leaders, advisors, governors and parents and in all sectors of education, to include:

- INSET
- Conferences
- Student Events
- Consultancy
- Books
- Podcasts

- Videocasts
- Learning Tools
- TV and Radio Broadcasts
- Articles
- Learning Technologies

To find out more and to access a wide range of free resources please check out www.independentthinking.co.uk.

The Independent Thinking Series of books is the latest in a line of innovative resources to help teachers and schools address the many challenges of the 21st century:

The Big Book of Independent Thinking: *Do things no one does or do things everyone does in a way no one does* — Edited by Ian Gilbert
A 'bible' for teachers with ideas and inspiration from many of our Associates across a wide range of topics. — ISBN 978-190442438-3

Little Owl's Book of Thinking: *An Introduction to Thinking Skills* — Ian Gilbert
An introduction to thinking, learning and living for younger children.
— ISBN 978-190442435-2

The Little Book of Thunks: *260 questions to make your brain go ouch!* — Ian Gilbert
Contagious philosophical questions to get young people's brains to hurt.
— ISBN 978-184590062-5

The Buzz: *A practical confidence builder for teenagers* — David Hodgson
Strategies for helping young people know themselves better for improved motivation, communication and success in school and beyond. — ISBN 978-190442481-9

The Learner's Toolkit: *Developing Emotional Intelligence, Instilling Values for Life, Creating Independent Learners and Supporting the SEAL Framework for Secondary Schools* —
Jackie Beere Edited by Ian Gilbert
Every teacher's essential guide to creating truly independent learners, confident and resilient in their ability to learn and learn well. — ISBN 978-184590070-0

Essential Motivation in the Classroom
An entertaining and inspiring read full of useful, practical advice on how to motivate children and how children can learn to motivate themselves. — ISBN 978-041526619-2

The Little Book of Big Stuff about the Brain: *The true story of your amazing brain* —
Andrew Curran Edited by Ian Gilbert
The brain has never been easier to comprehend. With the help of Andrew Curran's witty prose and illustrations, you will come to understand how the brain works and the implications this has for learning. — ISBN 978-184590085-4

Turning Your School Inside Out: *How to create an outstanding school through inspirational leadership* — Will Ryan Edited by Ian Gilbert
Will Ryan turns the issue of leadership in schools inside out . With his assistance schools will learn to ignore impositions from outside in favour of finding their true purpose.
— ISBN 978-184590084-7

www.independentthinking.co.uk   www.crownhouse.co.uk